Vegan Slow Cooker for Beginners

Vegan Slow Cooker

for Beginners

ESSENTIALS TO GET STARTED

ROCKRIDGE
PRESS

Contents

Introduction   1

CHAPTER ONE

What You Need to Know to Get Cooking   5

CHAPTER TWO

Shortcuts to Add to Your Slow-Cooking Success   17

CHAPTER THREE

Breakfasts   29

CHAPTER FOUR

Snacks, Sides, and Appetizers   45

CHAPTER FIVE

Soups   65

CHAPTER SIX

Stews and Chilies   97

CHAPTER SEVEN

Beans and Grains   125

CHAPTER EIGHT

Vegetables   151

CHAPTER NINE

Meat Alternatives   175

CHAPTER TEN

International Cuisine   201

CHAPTER ELEVEN

Desserts   223

Index   239

Introduction

This cookbook was created for vegans who are looking for new ways to prepare healthful foods. If you're often too tired to cook fresh vegan meals after a long day, you'll find that slow cooking gives you the flexibility to put your ingredients in a pot, go off to work, and come home to a delicious finished meal.

Slow cookers are usually associated with cooking stews and soups containing meat, and once you became a vegan you probably put yours away as a statement. If you've never used your slow cooker for preparing vegan foods, you may have simply lacked the slow-cooker recipes you needed.

So get out your slow cooker and wash it well. If you don't already own one, read chapter 1 for a guide to choosing the right slow cooker for your needs. This book will give you the know-how and recipes you need to create delicious, nutritious vegan meals in a whole new way.

THE ADVANTAGES OF SLOW COOKING

Cooking vegan meals, just like any other meals, can be time-consuming, and sometimes meal preparation is not what you want to deal with after a busy day at work or an exhausting outing with the kids. That's where your slow cooker comes in handy.

Here are just some of the advantages of slow-cooking vegan food:

- **Convenience.** You can cook when you have the time and schedule your meals accordingly. Some recipes involve a little preparation, while others require simply throwing your ingredients into the slow cooker, turning it on, and walking away.
- **Vital nutrients are retained.** The micronutrients that are necessary for strengthening your immune system and fighting chronic diseases remain in foods when you prepare them in a slow cooker, thanks to the lower cooking temperature.
- **Richer flavors.** Cooking slower and longer makes the already satisfying flavors in plant-based foods even more delicious.

- **A complete meal in a pot.** A slow cooker produces food that can be taken directly to your table or on the road to share at a potluck or a holiday spread.

Slow cookers can easily prepare all the foods you are used to eating as a vegan: 100 percent plant-based foods such as fruits, vegetables, whole grains, and beans. The recipes in this book include the following mouth-watering choices:

- Pumpkin Cinnamon Rolls
- Black Bean Breakfast Burritos
- Mashed Cauliflower and Garlic "Potatoes"
- Alphabet Minestrone
- "Meaty" Shiitake Stew
- Ratatouille Niçoise
- Enchilada Wraps

You can even use the slow cooker to prepare vegan desserts. Chocolate–Peanut Butter Cake (page 234) is just one of the satisfying dessert recipes in this book.

The majority of these recipes focus on real vegan foods, with chapter 9 set aside for recipes using meat alternatives, namely, tofu, tempeh, and seitan. These are minimally processed foods that act as meat substitutes in many traditional dishes, such as lasagna, beef stroganoff, and sloppy joes.

Tofu and tempeh are soy-based products. Both foods are staples in parts of Asia and are excellent sources of a variety of nutrients, including protein. Finding these foods is no longer a challenge; they are sold in health food stores and most supermarkets.

Tofu, also known as bean curd, is made by coagulating soy milk and pressing the resulting curds into square forms, where it drains to varying degrees of firmness. Tofu is very mild; like pasta, it absorbs the flavors of the other foods it is prepared with. Tofu is what makes Barbecue-Style Tofu and Pineapple (page 180) a must for any cookout.

Tempeh is a fermented soy product that comes in the form of a very firm cake. Unlike tofu, tempeh has a distinctive nutty flavor all its own. Tempeh helps give the Tempeh Enchilada Casserole (page 187) its texture and substance.

Seitan, often referred to as "wheat meat," is a savior for those vegans allergic to soy. Just like tofu and tempeh, seitan originates from Asia and provides a variety of nutrients, including protein, but instead of being soy-based it is made from wheat gluten. Seitan can also be found easily wherever you shop.

Better yet, you can make your own right in the slow cooker—as you'll learn in chapter 2. Consider making the Chunky Seitan Roast (page 192) the centerpiece of your next dinner party.

FINAL THOUGHTS

Society as a whole is moving toward healthier, more sustainable foods. The most healthful and sustainable diet of all is one that is plant-based—or, more specifically, vegan. Finding new ways to prepare vegan foods offers you with more variety in your diet and more options for how to cook healthful and sustainable meals. Slow cooking can open up a whole new world of vegan enjoyment.

CHAPTER ONE

What You Need to Know to Get Cooking

What You Need to Know to Get Cooking

A slow cooker can be one of your best friends in the kitchen thanks to its versatility. Vegan slow cooking simply requires a little bit of knowledge before you get started.

GETTING STARTED

The number one concern with cooking in general is your safety and the safety of your loved ones. Even though a slow cooker utilizes no more energy than a 60-watt lightbulb, this appliance does get hot, inside and out. (However, it doesn't give off a lot of heat, making it a good choice for cooking in warm weather, when a conventional oven would make your kitchen hot and uncomfortable.) Keep the cooker and its cord out of sight and out of reach of small children. Like a conventional oven, the slow cooker should be a no-kid zone unless they are closely supervised.

Don't leave your slow cooker on when you are going out until you have checked it for safety. This applies to both a brand-new slow cooker and an older model you may have had for a while. Keep the slow cooker under a watchful eye the first time you use it, or the first time you use it after a long period of disuse. Anything electrical can malfunction, and this simple action will give you peace of mind.

When the slow cooker is not in use, unplug it. A slow cooker accidentally turned on when empty can lead to a cracked insert.

A slow cooker cooks food at a lower temperature than a conventional oven. A cooker that doesn't heat up as it should can be a safety concern because of the possibility of bacterial growth. There is a danger zone for foods, a temperature range within which certain foods (usually animal products) should not be kept for any length of time. Since all the foods you're cooking are vegan, the only real risk comes from food items that were contaminated before you purchased them.

If your slow cooker is fairly new, temperature is probably not a concern. With an older model, testing the temperature is a good idea. Here's an easy way to check: Leave 2 quarts water out at room temperature when you go to bed. In the morning, pour the water into your slow cooker and turn it on low for 8 hours. As soon as the lid comes off, check the temperature of the water with an instant-read thermometer. The temperature should be at least 185°F. If it is cooler than that, discard the cooker. In fact, if your slow cooker is old, it's probably time to invest in a new one.

BUYING THE RIGHT SLOW COOKER FOR YOU

Slow cookers come in a variety of models, some very basic, others with more bells and whistles. If budget is a concern, there are plenty of slow cookers on the market for under $100, including some that start at about $30.

Slow cookers come in different sizes and are either round or oval; shape does not affect the way the appliance works. All slow cookers use indirect heat at a low temperature for a long period of time. The coils at the base of the slow cooker generate the heat necessary for cooking but never come into direct contact with the food.

Small slow cookers range in size from 1½ to 3 quarts, ideal for small families or for when you want to prepare dips and fondues. A 4- to 5-quart slow cooker is considered a medium cooker and is perfect for a family of four. The larger slow cookers are 6, 7, and 8 quarts, and are invaluable when you need to cook for a big family or for social gatherings.

Having a variety of sizes of slow cookers is ideal but not necessary. A great alternative is a 3-in-1 model. A versatile piece of kitchen equipment, this cooker comes with 2-, 4-, and 6-quart inserts and is very affordable.

The recipes in this book are designed for a 4- to 5-quart slow cooker. Any recipe can be adjusted according to your needs. Check your slow cooker's manual for the optimal amount of food to put into the insert. This can vary, but is usually when the insert is between one-half and three-quarters full. It's much better to underfill than overfill a slow cooker.

You've selected the size, now what about the model? This really comes down to personal preference. Slow cooker options include the following:

- Removable metal inserts that can be used on the stove top. This eliminates the need for a skillet when browning vegetables.
- Removable ceramic inserts that may or may not be transferable to the stove top. A skillet may be necessary for browning vegetables.
- A baking insert, cooking rack, and temperature probe.
- Oversized handles, a locking lid, and an insulated carrying tote for travel.
- Programmable timer and temperature controls, with an option for the slow cooker to automatically turn off or revert to warm.

No matter which model you decide to purchase, slow cookers are easy to clean. Always let your slow cooker cool down before cleaning, and never submerge the electrical base of your slow cooker in water. Cleaning your slow cooker simply requires washing the insert with warm soapy water, rinsing it, and allowing it to air-dry. Wipe down the outside of the unit with a damp cloth and you're done.

WHAT YOU NEED TO KNOW ABOUT YOUR SLOW COOKER

There is some variation among different models, so you need to get to know your slow cooker on a personal level. Most of the recipes in this book provide a range of cooking times, e.g., cook on high for one to two hours. The age of your cooker is a factor here as well as the model. Older cookers generally cook at higher temperatures, while newer cookers operate at lower temperatures. Depending on the slow cooker and the recipe, you may need to adjust liquids as well as cooking times. When you determine the cooking time and amount of liquids that work best for a new recipe, don't hesitate to write the information down in this cookbook.

A WORD ABOUT SERVING SIZES

It is almost impossible for one slow cooker recipe to work perfectly for every slow cooker out there. The same can be said about serving sizes. A serving size for one person may be two servings for another or only half a serving for someone else. As you become more familiar with slow cooking and slow-cooking recipes, you will have a better understanding of what a recipe actually yields for you and your family.

THICKENERS

Adjusting liquids is a skill you will easily learn as you use your slow cooker more and more. Slow cookers are good at collecting moisture because of their enclosed method of cooking. When this moisture results in a dish that has too much liquid, one method of compensating is to set the slow cooker to high, being careful not to burn the food, and removing the lid until the liquid is absorbed (usually around 30 minutes).

If you don't have that much time or would like a different approach, there are several alternative methods you can try.

Adding puréed vegetables is a tried and true cooking technique. Potatoes work well here, but any vegetable will do. Simply scoop out approximately 1 cup of cooked vegetables from the slow cooker (more or less depending on the size of the dish), or use extra cooked potatoes if you have them. Purée the vegetables in a blender or food processor and stir the mixture into the slow cooker to thicken. Cooked rice is also a great thickener and will help decrease the amount of liquid in the slow cooker.

You can also add a small amount of water to a variety of different thickening ingredients to create a thickener that will effectively reduce the amount of liquid in the slow cooker. These are the three most common thickening ingredients:

- **Arrowroot:** Mix 1 tablespoon arrowroot with 2 tablespoons cold water per 2 cups liquid.

- **Cornstarch:** Mix 1 tablespoon cornstarch with 2 tablespoons cold water per 1 cup liquid.

- **Tapioca starch:** Mix 1 tablespoon tapioca starch with 2 tablespoons cold water per 2 cups liquid.

Again, simply stir the mixture into the slow cooker, cover the food, and turn the cooker to high for 10 minutes.

Fat and flour can be used to thicken your food, too. For this method, add 2 tablespoons all-purpose flour to 2 tablespoons melted vegan margarine on the stovetop. Stir for 1 minute, and then add ½ cup liquid from the slow cooker. Pour the mixture back into the slow cooker, stir, cover, and set on high for 10 minutes.

VEGGIE PREP AND VEGGIE TIPS

Cooking with a slow cooker will allow you to become skilled at time management and veggie preparation. Plan ahead using what works with your schedule to prep veggies ahead of time. Just store the prepped veggies in the refrigerator, ready to be pulled out when needed.

Precooking veggies, such as sautéing onions and garlic, is an excellent approach to adding even more flavor to whatever you are cooking. If you're pressed for time, just throw in the ingredients according to the recipe directions and move on. Vegetables release their natural liquids no matter how they are cooked.

The only exception to this approach is when you are cooking a stew. Stews use smaller amounts of liquid than other recipes. Under these circumstances, harder vegetables won't cook in the same amount of time as softer vegetables. In order to ensure equally cooked vegetables, precooking these harder vegetables is mandatory.

Root vegetables should always be peeled prior to cooking. These vegetables should also be cut into small uniform pieces in order to ensure they are thoroughly cooked when the rest of the ingredients they are combined with are ready to eat.

Softer veggies, such as bell peppers and zucchini, do not need to be cut into pieces that are quite as small as root vegetables pieces, but should still be uniform in size.

HERBS IN THE SLOW COOKER

Herbs, whether fresh or dried, represent a special scenario in slow cooking. Fresh herbs can lose some of their flavor when added at the beginning of the cooking process, whereas dried herbs can become too strong or even bitter. This is why seasonings are used sparingly in the slow cooker and should be added in the final minutes of cooking or even right before serving.

The recipes in this book specify which type of herb to use, but you can always substitute dry for fresh and vice versa. In general, 1 tablespoon of chopped fresh herbs equals 1 teaspoon of dried herbs.

ADDITIONAL INGREDIENTS AND KITCHEN TOOLS TO HAVE ON HAND

- Knives
- Sea salt
- Blender
- Cutting board
- Food processor
- Measuring cups
- Measuring spoons
- Vegetable peelers
- Nonstick cooking spray
- A variety of herbs and spices
- Pepper grinder
- Handheld immersion blender for puréeing soup
- Flaxseeds and flaxseed grinder or ground flaxseeds (used as an egg substitute)

A word about egg replacers: A number of ingredients can substitute for eggs in a vegan diet. The best substitution to use for the recipes in this book is either a store-bought egg substitute powder or ground flaxseeds. To replace 1 egg, you need 1 tablespoon of ground flaxseeds and 3 tablespoons of warm water. Stir the two ingredients together until they form a thick, gelatinous mixture.

ABOUT MEAT ALTERNATIVES

Tofu, tempeh, and seitan were mentioned briefly in the introduction. Seitan will be addressed further in chapter 2, when you learn how to make "wheat meat" in the slow cooker.

Tofu and tempeh are both soybean products that are used as meat alternatives in vegan cooking. Both foods take on the flavors of the foods they are prepared with. The nutritional value of these soy products was touched on earlier. A more in-depth look explains why tofu and tempeh are valuable additions to any slow-cooked vegan meal.

Tofu and Tempeh

Tofu is a good to excellent source of the recommended daily intake for magnesium, phosphorus, copper, selenium, omega-3 fatty acids, iron, manganese, calcium, and tryptophan. A 4-ounce serving of tofu supplies almost 20 percent of the daily value (DV) for protein at a cost of only 86 calories.

Tempeh is an excellent sources of the DV for magnesium, phosphorus, copper, manganese, and vitamin B2. Tempeh knocks tofu out of the protein park by supplying over 40 percent of the DV for protein in a 4-ounce serving. Tempeh comes with a higher caloric cost at 222 calories; still, it's a reasonable trade-off.

Types of Tofu

Tofu comes in a variety of textures (soft, medium, firm, and extra-firm) and in two forms: silken (Japanese-style) tofu or regular (Chinese-style) tofu.

Silken tofu is the softer of the two types of tofu and requires delicate handling. This tofu is typically found in 12-ounce aseptic boxes that do not need to be refrigerated. The texture of this tofu makes it well suited to making salad dressings, sauces, and desserts.

Regular tofu requires refrigeration and is packed in water in 14- or 16-ounce tubs. This tofu's texture is great for stir-fries and certain recipes in the slow cooker. Regular tofu can be precooked and added in at a late stage of the cooking process or combined with other ingredients to keep it from becoming too mushy or liquefied in the slow cooker.

All tofu contains water, and in order for the tofu to take on the flavors in the slow cooker, you must extract this water. Draining and squeezing the tofu may suffice; however, when you really want to extract as much water as possible from the tofu, it is a good idea to press it. Pressing is simple and can be done while you get your other ingredients ready:

1. Rinse the tofu under cool water.
2. Pat the tofu dry with paper towels.
3. Place the block of tofu on a plate.
4. Place another plate on top of the tofu.
5. Place several canned goods on top of the second plate to weigh it down. Press for as long as is feasible. Some cooks press their tofu anywhere from an hour to overnight.

Here is an even quicker method:

1. Cut the block of tofu in half horizontally.
2. Place the halves on four paper towels.
3. Cover the halves with four more paper towels.
4. Place the canned goods on top of the tofu for a few minutes.

Recipes in this book will specify what type of tofu to use and may refer to the "Prepared to Cook" method outlined below. This is the ideal method to get the most satisfaction out of cooking with tofu in your slow cooker. It involves freezing the tofu after pressing it. Freezing results in tofu that has a nuttier flavor, absorbs the flavors of other foods more effectively, and takes on a denser texture and consistency. This method should be used only with firm or extra-firm tofu, as less firm tofu will not freeze well.

The "Prepared to Cook" Method for Tofu

1. Drain the water from the tofu package.
2. Press the tofu as instructed above.
3. Place the tofu in an airtight plastic bag. Place the plastic bag in the freezer for at least 24 hours (or up to 3 months). You will notice that the tofu turns dark yellow when frozen. There is nothing wrong with the tofu; it will return to its original color after thawing.
4. When you are ready to use the tofu, thaw the tofu in the microwave, on the counter, or in the refrigerator. Thawing tofu in the refrigerator is the least effective approach unless the tofu is sliced before freezing.
5. Squeeze out any excess water from the tofu.
6. Cook the tofu according to the recipe instructions.

Tempeh

Tempeh and the slow cooker were made for each other. Unlike tofu, tempeh's hearty, chewy texture means it is easily adaptable for a variety of recipes. It's perfect for Portobello Mushroom and Tempeh Stroganoff (page 189) or Peanut, Tempeh, and Butternut Squash Mole (page 185). The only drawback to using tempeh in the slow cooker is it can sometimes seem bitter to certain people. If this is something you experience, simply steam the tempeh for ten minutes before adding it to the slow cooker. Tempeh can be used in its plain soy version; if you feel like experimenting, you can try three-grain tempeh, flax tempeh, smoky tempeh, or any other available flavors. Tempeh can be stored in the refrigerator or the freezer.

MORE SLOW COOKER TIPS

It's really tempting, but don't lift the lid on your slow cooker unless the recipe specifically calls for stirring or you need to add extra seasonings during the cooking process. You may need to add 15 to 20 minutes more cooking time for each time you lift the lid, so do it quickly.

As a general rule of thumb, it is much better to cook less food in a larger slow cooker than to cook more food in a smaller one. Increase the cooking time if the cooker is very full; decrease the cooking time if the cooker is not as full.

Never add cold food to an empty preheated slow cooker as the dramatic temperature change may cause the insert to crack.

Nonstick cooking spray can be used in any recipe where you feel its use is warranted. Even though specific recipes call for using nonstick cooking spray and other recipes don't, it's fine to go ahead and use the spray whenever you feel the need.

Some foods, such as spinach and pasta, can't withstand a lot of cooking. In those cases, simply precook the food in question with your desired method and add the item or items at the end of the slow-cooking process.

A FINAL TIP

Do you live at more than 3,000 feet above sea level? When living at such a high altitude, it is necessary to cook foods in the slow cooker on high for a longer period of time due to the lower atmospheric pressure. Under these circumstances, water comes to a boil more quickly and at a lower temperature. You may also need to increase liquids slightly, as the lower pressure leads to an increase in evaporation. The low setting can be used to keep foods warm.

Shortcuts to Add to Your Slow-Cooking Success

CHAPTER 2

Shortcuts to Add to Your Slow-Cooking Success

Mastering the art of vegan slow cooking comes from practice and from implementing the tricks of experienced slow cookers. These tricks will allow you to get ahead of your favorite recipes by being fully armed with the basics.

As you read through this book you will find recipes that call for some of the same basic building blocks. These foods can easily be prepared ahead of time and even refrigerated or frozen for use at a later date. Slow-cooker shortcuts will assist you in saving time—and sometimes even money.

You might want to learn how to make the following basic recipes before you get started on the other 150 recipes in this book:

- Beans
- Rice
- Seitan
- Vegetable Broth Bouillon Cubes
- Vegetable Stock

STOCK VERSUS BROTH

Stock and broth are differentiated in the meat-eating world primarily by the amount of meat involved. Broth generally involves cooking meats or fish with vegetables, while stock comes from cooking meaty bones, which produce gelatin, with vegetables.

In the vegan world, the difference between a vegetable stock and a vegetable broth is simple. A stock is typically unseasoned and is not usually a food consumed on its own, whereas a broth is typically heartier and more seasoned, and can be consumed on its own.

STOCK

The definition of the word "stock" gives another clue about the differences between stock and a broth. Stock is described as "a supporting framework or structure." In terms of cooking, a stock is used as part of a recipe to support the primary ingredients.

A vegetable stock is made by simmering vegetables with the purpose of extracting their flavor and using the resulting liquid as a base for other foods. Vegetable stock can be used in soups, for braising other vegetables, or in rice dishes such as risotto.

The great thing about making a good vegetable stock is that you can use whatever you have left over from prepping veggies for your recipes. Ideal ingredients for stock include carrot peelings, onion and garlic skins, celery leaves and ends, and parsley stems.

Vegetable Stock

Save your vegetable scraps in a zip-top bag in the freezer. Then, when you have a good amount stored up, you're ready to make a big batch of vegetable stock.

Miscellaneous vegetable scraps and ends, thoroughly washed
Water, as needed to cover vegetables

1. Place the vegetable scraps in the slow cooker.
2. Add enough water to completely cover the vegetables.
3. Cover and cook on low for 10 to 12 hours.
4. Place a colander in a large stockpot.
5. Carefully strain the stock and discard the vegetable scraps.
6. Cool the vegetable stock completely.
7. Store the vegetable stock in freezer-safe containers until you are ready to use.

BROTH AND BOUILLON CUBES

Vegetable broth can simply be thought as a seasoned vegetable stock. The broth has more flavor and substance than a stock. Remember eating vegetable broth as a kid when you were home sick from school? A vegetable stock would not have been nearly as tasty.

Most recipes for stocks are actually recipes for broths. The vegetable stock recipe in this chapter is truly a recipe for vegetable stock. For consistency, the recipes in this book specify the use of vegetable stock.

The recipes for vegetable stock and vegetable broth (in the form bouillon cubes) in this chapter can be used interchangeably in many recipes. Some experimentation may be necessary to discover your preference. Instead of vegetable stock, you can use an equal amount of water and one or two vegetable bouillon cubes, and omit the salt from the recipe.

Vegetable Broth Bouillon Cubes
MAKES 3 TO 4 CUPS

Who needs canned vegetable broth when you can make your own vegetable broth bouillon cubes? When you want something a little heartier than vegetable stock, this bouillon comes in handy. Each individual bouillon cube equals approximately 2 tablespoons and can be used, with water, just like broth.

Nonstick cooking spray
4 medium carrots, chopped
4 celery stalks, chopped
2 large yellow onions, quartered
1 cup water
2 teaspoons dried thyme
2 teaspoons dried parsley
1 teaspoon cracked black pepper, or to taste
1 teaspoon sea salt, or to taste
1 cup nutritional yeast

1. Lightly spray the slow cooker with the nonstick cooking spray.
2. Combine the carrots, celery, yellow onions, water, thyme, parsley, black pepper, and sea salt in the slow cooker.
3. Cover and cook on low for 8 to 12 hours.
4. When the broth is ready, pour it into a blender or food processor.
5. Add the nutritional yeast and purée.
6. Store up to a week's supply of broth in a covered container in the refrigerator.
7. Pour the rest of the broth into ice cube trays and place in the freezer.
8. When the broth has formed solid cubes, remove the cubes from the trays.
9. Put the cubes in a large freezer bag and store in the freezer for later use.

RICE

Rice is another staple in the vegan diet, and knowing how to cook it properly is a real asset. You will have the best results with cooking rice in the slow cooker if you cook it as a separate dish. Converted rice and Arborio rice (used for risotto) are the two exceptions to this scenario. These types of rice can be added to a recipe uncooked and will provide the results you are looking for.

Other types of rice, due to their thickening properties, alter recipes by absorbing too much of the liquid in the slow cooker. Cooked rice can be added at the end of the cooking process or served on the side with a slow-cooked meal.

Cooking rice in the slow cooker has some advantages:

* No more burned rice
* No boiled-over messes
* Consistently fluffy rice

Three basic rice recipes provided here will be used throughout the book to accompany different types of meals. These are your kitchen's staple recipes.

Slow-Cooked Brown Basmati Rice
MAKES 3 CUPS

This is the preferred brown rice for the slow cooker. Basmati rice is a real treat and means "queen of fragrance." A long-grain rice with a nutty aroma, this finely textured rice is grown in the Himalayas and Pakistan. When cooking basmati rice, it is imperative not to open the lid of the slow cooker within the first two hours of cooking.

Nonstick cooking spray
2 cups vegetable stock (page 20)
1 cup uncooked brown basmati rice
1 tablespoon sea salt

1. Spray the slow cooker generously with the nonstick cooking spray.
2. Combine the vegetable stock, brown rice, and sea salt in the slow cooker and stir well.
3. Cover and cook on low for 2 hours.
4. Check the rice for tenderness. If needed, continue to cook the rice for an additional 20 minutes, or until done.

5. When the rice is done, turn the slow cooker to warm.

6. Serve when ready.

Pilaf-Style Rice
MAKES 4 ½ CUPS

Converted rice, also known as parboiled rice, is rice that falls somewhere between brown rice and white rice nutritionally. This type of rice undergoes a steaming process before it is husked, allowing the rice to absorb some of the nutrients it would otherwise lose. After cooking, converted rice retains more nutrients and is firmer and less sticky than white rice, making it ideal for the slow cooker.

1 ¾ cups vegetable stock (page 20)

⅔ cup water

Nonstick cooking spray

1 ½ cups converted long-grain rice

½ cup thinly sliced carrot

¼ teaspoon cracked black pepper

1. Combine the vegetable stock and water in a 4-cup glass measuring cup and microwave on high until very hot, about 5 minutes.

2. Lightly spray the slow cooker with the nonstick cooking spray.

3. Combine the rice, carrot, and black pepper in the slow cooker and stir.

4. Pour the hot liquid into the slow cooker.

5. Cover and cook on high for 1 ½ to 2 hours, or until the rice is tender.

6. Serve when ready.

Arborio Rice
MAKES 3 CUPS

Arborio rice is best known for its use in risotto and rice pudding. An Italian short-grain rice, Arborio becomes firm and chewy after cooking. This rice is also on the creamy side due to its high starch content. When using this rice as an accompaniment to certain dishes, you may want to omit the shallot or cheese.

2 tablespoons vegan margarine, melted

1 shallot, minced (optional)

1 cup Arborio rice

3 cups vegetable stock (page 20)

Grated vegan Parmesan cheese (optional)

1. Combine the vegan margarine, shallot (if using), and rice in the slow cooker and stir.
2. Pour in the vegetable stock.
3. Cover and cook on high for 2 hours, or until most of the liquid has been absorbed.
4. Sprinkle with Parmesan (if using) and serve when ready.

OTHER GRAINS

There are recipes in this book that use other types of grains, such as millet. Simply cook these grains according to the directions and you will get good results.

Slow-Cooked Seitan
MAKES 4 BALLS

Seitan is a wheat product that tastes like meat. It's not surprising that seitan is used as a meat alternative in many recipes, including several in this book. Seitan prepared in the slow cooker can be used right away or stored for up to ten days in the refrigerator and as long as six months in the freezer.

2 ½ cups vital wheat gluten flour
⅓ cup nutritional yeast
¼ teaspoon cracked black pepper
2 cups water
3 tablespoons soy sauce
2 tablespoons olive oil
1 yellow onion, coarsely chopped
6 garlic cloves, coarsely chopped
1 teaspoon dried thyme
1 teaspoon dried rosemary
1 teaspoon dried sage
4 cups vegetable stock (page 20)

1. In a large mixing bowl, whisk together the wheat gluten flour, nutritional yeast, and black pepper until well combined.
2. Stir in the water, soy sauce, and olive oil until a dough is formed.
3. Knead the dough for 1 to 2 minutes.

4. Let the dough rest for 5 minutes.

5. Preheat the slow cooker to low.

6. Cut the dough into 4 pieces.

7. Shape each piece of dough into a ball.

8. Arrange the seitan dough balls in the bottom of the slow cooker.

9. Sprinkle the onion, garlic, thyme, rosemary, and sage over the dough.

10. Pour the vegetable stock over the dough.

11. Cover and cook on low for 6 to 8 hours.

12. Turn off the slow cooker. Let the seitan cool in the slow cooker until it is cool enough to handle, about 1 hour.

13. Place the seitan and the vegetable stock in a container with a tightly fitting lid. Make sure the vegetable stock covers the seitan completely. Alternately, remove the seitan from the vegetable stock and wrap the seitan tightly in plastic wrap. Store the seitan in the refrigerator or freezer.

BEANS

Beans are a staple in almost every vegan's diet. Beans come in an assortment of sizes, colors, and flavors. They are a health-supporting food and are packed with a wide variety of nutrients. The Black Bean Soup (page 85) in particular provides an excellent source of protein, fiber, folate, and iron. When the black beans and tomatoes in this soup are combined, iron intake is increased even more.

Brazil and India produce more black beans than any other country. These beans are popular in the United States and are highly recommended by a multitude of respected health organizations due to their association with lower risks of many forms of chronic conditions such as type 2 diabetes, cardiovascular disease, and certain kinds of cancer.

The recipes in this book call for canned beans but can just as easily be made with soaked and cooked dried beans. If you are on a budget, you already know how much more economical dried beans are. Whatever your preference, the recipes will work just as well with either one. Here is a simple formula for converting from one type to another:

½ cup dried beans = 1½ cups cooked beans = 1 (15-ounce) can of beans

Soaking Dried Beans: Why Should You?

Soaking is a personal preference and certainly not mandatory but definitely a practice you should be aware of and strongly consider using. Soaking decreases the amount of starches (sugar) present in the beans and limits the amount of intestinal distress you may otherwise experience from eating them. Soaking also decreases cooking time and may even lead to better-tasting beans. Lentils and split peas do not require soaking.

The Soaking Process

Before soaking, rinse the dried beans thoroughly and drain in a colander. Pick out any imperfect beans and any rocks or pebbles that may be present. Soak the beans in three times their volume of cold water. The tendency to oversoak beans can be strong, but 6 hours is all that is needed.

When you're short of time, try the quick-soaking method:

1. Place the beans in a pot and cover with cold water.
2. Slowly bring the water to a boil.
3. Remove the pot from the heat and let the beans soak in the water for 1 to 2 hours.

Slow-Cooked Beans

1. Pour 4 cups of water into the slow cooker if you are cooking 1 cup of soaked beans. Use 6 cups of water for 2 cups of beans.
2. Turn the slow cooker on high and add the beans. Cover the slow cooker. Cook the beans according to the following time guidelines:

   - Lentils: 1½ to 2 hours
   - Split peas: 2½ hours
   - Great northern and navy beans: 2½ to 3 hours
   - Black, cannellini, kidney, and pinto beans: 3 hours
   - Black-eyed peas: 3½ hours
   - Chickpeas: 4 hours

3. An hour before the beans are to finish cooking, check the water level. If the beans are not completely submerged, add enough boiling water to cover them.

4. After the beans are completely cooked, turn off the slow cooker. Allow the beans to remain in the slow cooker while they cool, and then drain them in a strainer or colander. (When beans are cooked, they release an indigestible sugar, or oligosaccharide, into the water. This sugar is responsible for the gas and intestinal distress that often accompanies a good bean dish. Draining the beans allows most of the sugar to be discarded along with the water.)

5. Use the beans right away or store them in the refrigerator or freezer.

IMPORTANT: Cannellini and kidney beans must be boiled for fifteen minutes prior to slow cooking. Both beans contain the natural toxin lectin phytohemagglutinin, which may not be adequately destroyed in a slow cooker.

Breakfasts

PUMPKIN CINNAMON ROLLS

EXTRA-CREAMY TAPIOCA PUDDING

BANANA QUINOA BREAKFAST

AMARANTH AND FRUIT

PUMPKIN GINGERBREAD CEREAL

COCONUTTY OATS

SUPER-SLOW TART APPLE AND
   CINNAMON OATMEAL

CHOCOLATY STEEL-CUT OATS

HASH-BROWN CASSEROLE

BLACK BEAN BREAKFAST BURRITOS

CHAPTER THREE

Breakfasts

Pumpkin Cinnamon Rolls

MAKES 12 TO 14 ROLLS

There is nothing like the smell of baked goods drifting from your oven. Anticipation builds; you actually start salivating thinking about how good that first bite is going to be. The same experience can be had with your slow cooker, too. In this case the aromas are of pumpkin, cinnamon, nutmeg, ginger, and cloves—it smells like a pumpkin pie.

FOR THE ROLLS:

NONSTICK COOKING SPRAY

3 CUPS ALL-PURPOSE FLOUR

¼ CUP GRANULATED SUGAR

1 (¼-OUNCE) PACKAGE ACTIVE DRY YEAST

¾ CUP CANNED PUMPKIN PURÉE

½ CUP VANILLA ALMOND MILK

½ CUP CANOLA OIL

¼ CUP WATER

EGG SUBSTITUTE EQUIVALENT TO 1 EGG

FOR THE FILLING:

1 TO 2 TABLESPOONS ALL-PURPOSE FLOUR

⅓ CUP VEGAN MARGARINE, SOFTENED

⅓ CUP PACKED LIGHT BROWN SUGAR

2 TEASPOONS GROUND CINNAMON

2 TEASPOONS GROUND NUTMEG

1 TEASPOON GROUND GINGER

1 TEASPOON GROUND GLOVES

FOR THE ICING:

1 CUP POWDERED SUGAR

4 OUNCES VEGAN CREAM CHEESE, SOFTENED

¼ CUP VEGAN MARGARINE, SOFTENED

½ TEASPOON VANILLA EXTRACT

½ TEASPOON FRESH LEMON JUICE

continued ▶

Make the rolls:

1. Lightly spray the slow cooker with the nonstick cooking spray.

2. In a large bowl, combine the flour, sugar, and yeast.

3. Fold the pumpkin purée, almond milk, canola oil, water, and egg substitute into the dry ingredients.

4. Form the mixture into a ball in the bowl.

5. Cover the bowl with a towel and let it sit for 30 to 45 minutes.

Make the filling:

1. Lightly dust a kitchen surface with the flour.

2. Roll the dough ball into a rectangle on the lightly floured surface.

3. In a small bowl, combine the vegan margarine, brown sugar, cinnamon, nutmeg, ginger, and cloves to make the filling.

4. Cover the dough rectangle with the pumpkin spice filling.

5. Roll the dough lengthwise into a log and pinch the ends to seal.

6. Cut the log into 12 to 14 slices.

7. Place the slices in the slow cooker.

8. Cover and cook on high for 60 for 90 minutes. Poke a toothpick into the center of one of the rolls; if it comes out clean, your rolls are done.

Make the icing:

1. In a small bowl, mix the powdered sugar, vegan cream cheese, vegan margarine, vanilla extract, and lemon juice.

2. Pour the icing over the hot rolls.

3. Serve hot.

Extra-Creamy Tapioca Pudding

MAKES 6 SERVINGS

Tapioca pudding is a great treat for breakfast, especially if it's extra creamy. This pudding recipe is formulated for a 3- to 4-quart slow cooker. Simply double the recipe if you have a larger slow cooker. Serve with fresh blueberries and strawberries for a healthful morning wake-up call.

4 CUPS UNSWEETENED VANILLA COCONUT MILK

½ CUP SMALL PEARL TAPIOCA

2 TEASPOONS ORANGE EXTRACT

1 TEASPOON VANILLA EXTRACT

SWEETENER, TO TASTE (OPTIONAL)

1. Combine the coconut milk, pearl tapioca, orange extract, and vanilla extract in the slow cooker.

2. Cook on low for 3½ to 4½ hours or on high for approximately 2 hours.

3. Place the tapioca pudding in the refrigerator for several hours to firm up.

4. Add the desired sweetener (if using) and serve cold.

Banana Quinoa Breakfast

MAKES 4 SERVINGS

Quinoa is a staple of many vegan diets but is usually reserved for lunch or dinner. This recipe will change your mind about that. Quinoa is a complete protein source with an abundance of other nutrients. One cup of cooked quinoa provides 8 grams of protein, 5 grams of dietary fiber, and good amounts of folate, vitamin B6, thiamin, riboflavin, manganese, magnesium, phosphorus, iron, zinc, and copper. The bananas and walnuts are an added bonus, supplying potassium and omega-3 fatty acids.

1 CUP UNCOOKED QUINOA, RINSED

1 CUP WATER

½ CUP SOY COFFEE CREAMER

½ CUP SOY MILK

1½ TABLESPOONS VEGAN MARGARINE, MELTED

½ TEASPOON VANILLA EXTRACT

1½ TABLESPOONS GROUND CINNAMON

1½ VERY RIPE BANANAS

3 TABLESPOONS PACKED LIGHT BROWN SUGAR

2 TABLESPOONS CHOPPED WALNUTS

1 BANANA, SLICED (OPTIONAL)

1. Combine the quinoa, water, soy coffee creamer, soy milk, vegan margarine, vanilla extract, and cinnamon in the slow cooker.

2. In a small bowl, mash the very ripe bananas. Stir the mashed bananas into the ingredients in the slow cooker.

3. Sprinkle the brown sugar and walnuts over the quinoa mixture and stir, mixing thoroughly.

4. Cook on low for 4 to 6 hours, or until the quinoa is fully cooked.

5. Serve warm with banana slices, if desired.

Amaranth and Fruit

MAKES 4 SERVINGS

Amaranth is perfect for a gluten-free diet. This "grain" is actually a seed that was a diet staple for the Aztecs and Mayans. Amaranth is unique in its consistency and flavor. Slightly nutty, slightly malty, and similar to porridge, amaranth is a big hit for breakfast. In addition to the raisins and dates in this recipe, serve with granola and peaches for a sweeter and crunchier dish.

6 CUPS WATER

1½ CUPS AMARANTH

1 TEASPOON SEA SALT

¾ CUP RAISINS

¾ CUP CHOPPED DATES

½ TEASPOON GROUND CORIANDER

1. Turn the slow cooker on high.

2. Place 4 cups of the water, amaranth, and sea salt in a saucepan and bring to a boil.

3. Pour the boiling mixture into the slow cooker.

4. Cover immediately and reduce the heat to low.

5. Cook overnight.

6. Meanwhile, place the raisins and dates in a large bowl and add the remaining 2 cups water.

7. Leave the dried fruit to soak overnight.

8. In the morning, 15 minutes before serving the amaranth, add the soaked fruit, soaking water, and coriander to the slow cooker.

9. Stir and serve hot.

Pumpkin Gingerbread Cereal

MAKES 8 SERVINGS

A pumpkin gingerbread dessert can be easily converted to a breakfast food by serving it in a bowl and adding some vanilla soy milk—voilà, cereal in an instant. More pumpkin than ginger, this morning treat will help you start the day right, with your daily dose of beta carotene and the oomph that the pumpkin pie spices bring to your sleepy taste buds.

NONSTICK COOKING SPRAY

2 CUPS WHOLE-WHEAT PASTRY FLOUR

1½ TABLESPOONS GROUND GINGER

1 TABLESPOON BAKING POWDER

1 TEASPOON GROUND CINNAMON

½ TEASPOON BAKING SODA

½ TEASPOON GROUND CLOVES

½ TEASPOON GROUND ALLSPICE

¼ TEASPOON GROUND NUTMEG

¼ TEASPOON SEA SALT

2 TABLESPOONS GROUND FLAXSEEDS

2 TABLESPOONS WARM WATER

1 CUP CANNED PUMPKIN PURÉE

½ CUP MOLASSES

½ CUP MAPLE SYRUP

¼ CUP OLIVE OIL

1 TEASPOON VANILLA EXTRACT

VANILLA SOY MILK (OPTIONAL)

1. Lightly spray the slow cooker with the nonstick cooking spray.

2. In a large bowl, combine the pastry flour, ginger, baking powder, cinnamon, baking soda, cloves, allspice, nutmeg, and sea salt.

3. In a separate large bowl, mix the flaxseeds and warm water together.

4. Stir the pumpkin purée, molasses, maple syrup, olive oil, and vanilla into the flaxseed mixture.

5. Add the pastry flour mixture to the pumpkin mixture and stir with a wooden spoon until just combined.

6. Add the mixture to the slow cooker.

7. Vent the slow cooker during cooking by placing a wooden spoon across the top, under the lid.

8. Cook on high for 1 1/2 to 2 1/2 hours, or until a knife inserted into the center comes out clean.

9. Serve warm with vanilla soy milk, if desired.

Coconutty Oats

MAKES 4 TO 6 SERVINGS

Coconut has become very popular in the vegan community in the past few years. Could it be the taste? How about the coconut's medium-chain fatty acids? This type of fatty acids make the drupe (no, it's not a nut) an easily digestible food and a good choice for those with digestives concerns, including the elderly. The steel-cut oats provide the foundation for a powerhouse breakfast with a coconutty punch.

NONSTICK COOKING SPRAY

4 CUPS UNSWEETENED COCONUT MILK

1 CUP STEEL-CUT OATS

1 CUP FINELY SHREDDED UNSWEETENED COCONUT

2 TEASPOONS VANILLA EXTRACT

1 TEASPOON LEMON EXTRACT

2 TO 3 TABLESPOONS SWEETENER (OPTIONAL)

½ CUP VANILLA COCONUT MILK

1 TEASPOON COCONUT EXTRACT

1. Lightly spray the slow cooker with the nonstick cooking spray.

2. Combine the coconut milk, steel-cut oats, shredded coconut, vanilla extract, and lemon extract in the slow cooker and stir well.

3. Cook on low for 7 to 9 hours or overnight.

4. In the morning, stir the oatmeal well.

5. Stir in the sweetener of your choice.

6. Ladle the oatmeal into breakfast bowls.

7. To make the topping, combine the vanilla coconut milk and the coconut extract.

8. Pour some coconut topping on each serving.

9. Serve immediately.

Super-Slow Tart Apple and Cinnamon Oatmeal

MAKES 4 SERVINGS

Breakfast should be a relaxing time; however, with work, kids, and life in general, breakfast often gets overlooked. Those who skip breakfast are much more likely to carry around a few extra pounds and experience lower energy levels long before it's time to eat lunch. Oatmeal cooked overnight eliminates all of these concerns. Breakfast is ready and waiting when you wake up.

NONSTICK COOKING SPRAY

2 LARGE TART APPLES, PEELED, CORED, AND CHOPPED

1½ CUPS SOY MILK

1½ CUPS WATER

1 CUP WHOLE-GRAIN ROLLED OATS

3 TABLESPOONS PACKED DARK BROWN SUGAR

2 TABLESPOONS VEGAN MARGARINE, SOFTENED

1 TABLESPOON GROUND CINNAMON, OR TO TASTE

2 TABLESPOONS GROUND FLAXSEEDS

¼ TEASPOON SEA SALT

¼ CUP RAISINS OR DRIED CRANBERRIES (OPTIONAL)

¼ CUP CHOPPED NUTS (WALNUTS, ALMONDS, PECANS, OR A MIXTURE), IF DESIRED

1. Lightly spray the slow cooker with the nonstick cooking spray.

2. Combine the apples, soy milk, water, oats, dark brown sugar, vegan margarine, cinnamon, and flaxseeds in the slow cooker and stir well.

3. Cover and cook on low for 7 to 8 hours or overnight.

4. Stir the sea salt into the oatmeal just before serving.

5. Serve hot with dried fruit and nuts, if desired.

Chocolaty Steel-Cut Oats

MAKES 4 SERVINGS

Steel-cut oats, also known as Irish oats, are whole-grain groats (the inner portion of the oat kernel that has been cut into pieces). These oats have traditionally been used in Scotland and Ireland to make porridge, a cereal cooked with water or milk that is very similar to what we call oatmeal. Steel-cut oats are considered healthier than other types of oats due to their minimal processing. These oats are coarser in texture and provide real substance to a breakfast. Add a little chocolate and what else do you need?

NONSTICK COOKING SPRAY

4 CUPS WATER

½ CUP UNSWEETENED COCONUT MILK

2 TABLESPOONS MAPLE SYRUP

1 TEASPOON VANILLA EXTRACT

1 TABLESPOON UNSWEETENED COCOA POWDER

¼ TEASPOON SEA SALT

1 CUP STEEL-CUT OATS

SHAVED VEGAN CHOCOLATE (OPTIONAL)

1. Lightly spray the slow cooker with the nonstick cooking spray.

2. In a large bowl, combine the water, coconut milk, maple syrup, and vanilla.

3. Whisk in the cocoa powder and sea salt.

4. Stir in the oats.

5. Pour the mixture into the slow cooker.

6. Cover and cook on low for 1 to 2 hours.

7. Leave on warm overnight.

8. Stir the oatmeal in the morning.

9. Serve warm with shaved vegan chocolate, if desired.

Hash-Brown Casserole

MAKES 8 TO 10 SERVINGS

Hash browns are a tradition for breakfast, but not like this. This hash-brown casserole seems more like a game-day party breakfast. Serve with toast or an English muffin on the side. If you're feeling really adventurous, put the casserole right on top of the bread. (This is not the breakfast for you if you are watching your weight!)

NONSTICK COOKING SPRAY
2 POUNDS FROZEN HASH BROWN POTATOES
1 (12-OUNCE) CONTAINER SALSA
1 (12-OUNCE) CONTAINER VEGAN SOUR CREAM
1 GARLIC CLOVE, MINCED
1 (8-OUNCE) VEGAN JALAPEÑO-GARLIC CHEESE WEDGE,
    VERY THINLY SLICED
½ CUP UNSWEETENED ALMOND MILK

1. Lightly spray the slow cooker with the nonstick cooking spray.

2. Put the frozen hash brown potatoes in the slow cooker.

3. Turn the slow cooker on high.

4. Stir in the salsa, vegan sour cream, and garlic.

5. Stir in the vegan cheese.

6. Pour the almond milk over the potatoes.

7. Cover and cook for 2 hours.

8. Turn on low, remove the cover, and cook for 1 additional hour.

9. Serve hot.

Black Bean Breakfast Burritos

Black beans are a filling option for any meal, and breakfast is no exception. Black beans are hearty and a precursor to good digestion, the most important part of any meal. The indigestible fraction (IF for short) in these beans is higher than in many other types of beans. This level of IF lends support to a properly functioning digestive tract, especially the large intestine. Bacteria in the gut is kept in balance, and studies have shown a lower risk of colon cancer for those who regularly eat black beans.

2 CUPS VEGETABLE STOCK (PAGE 20)

1 (15-OUNCE) CAN BLACK BEANS, RINSED AND DRAINED

1 (10-OUNCE) CAN DICED TOMATOES WITH GREEN CHILES, UNDRAINED

1 CUP UNCOOKED PEARL BARLEY

¾ CUPS FROZEN CORN

¼ CUP CHOPPED SCALLIONS

3 GARLIC CLOVES, CHOPPED

1 TABLESPOON FRESH LIME JUICE

1 TEASPOON GROUND CUMIN

1 TEASPOON CHILI POWDER

½ TEASPOON CAYENNE PEPPER

6 FLOUR TORTILLAS, WARMED

SHREDDED VEGAN CHEDDAR CHEESE, CHOPPED FRESH CILANTRO,
    SALSA, SHREDDED LETTUCE, AND GUACAMOLE (OPTIONAL)

1. Combine the vegetable stock, black beans, tomatoes with their juices, pearl barley, corn, scallions, garlic, lime juice, cumin, chili powder, and pepper in the slow cooker and stir well.

2. Cover and cook on low for 4 to 5 hours.

3. Spread the burrito filling on the 6 flour tortillas, dividing evenly.

4. If desired, add the shredded vegan cheddar cheese, cilantro, salsa, lettuce, and guacamole to the tortillas.

5. Fold up the burritos and serve immediately.

CHAPTER FOUR

Snacks, Sides, and Appetizers

APRICOT BUTTER

HOME-STYLE APPLESAUCE

CURRIED ALMONDS

SPICY PECANS

NUTTY COCONUT CURRY MIX

ROOT VEGETABLES WITH OIL
   AND VINEGAR

SWEET ACORN SQUASH

STUFFED PICANTE ONIONS

SWEET POTATO CASSEROLE

MASHED CAULIFLOWER AND
   GARLIC "POTATOES"

TOMATO SALSA

MARINATED MUSHROOMS

SPICED INDIAN CHICKPEAS

NONTRADITIONAL ANTIPASTO

MEXICAN BEAN DIP

Snacks, Sides, and Appetizers

Apricot Butter

MAKES 3 CUPS

Fresh through the summer, smooth, sweet apricots have abundant beta carotene, making them a good source of vitamin A. With a distinctive flavor unlike any other fruit butter, this slow-cooked apricot butter hits the spot when spread on your favorite lightly toasted bread. When you've had your fill of apricots, substitute peaches.

2 (29-OUNCE) CANS APRICOT HALVES, DRAINED
1½ CUPS SUGAR
1 TEASPOON GROUND CINNAMON
½ TEASPOON GROUND CLOVES

1. Purée the apricots in a blender or food processor.

2. Pour the apricot purée into the slow cooker.

3. Stir in the sugar, cinnamon, and cloves.

4. Cover and cook on high for 4 to 5 hours.

5. Remove the cover and cook for an additional 4 to 5 hours, stirring occasionally.

6. Serve hot or cold.

Home-Style Applesauce

Applesauce is a light, healthful, and satisfying snack. The cinnamon adds a little kick; you can add a little extra on top of your serving. Research on cinnamon has found it to have antibacterial properties, decrease inflammation, and act as an antioxidant. But don't overdo it—high intakes of cinnamon can actually be toxic.

4 POUNDS TART APPLES, PEELED, CORED, AND THINLY SLICED
½ CUP SUGAR
½ TEASPOON GROUND CINNAMON
1 CUP WATER
1 TABLESPOON FRESH LEMON JUICE

1. Combine the apples, sugar, and cinnamon in the slow cooker and stir well.

2. Pour the water and lemon juice over the apples.

3. Cover and cook on low for 6 hours or on high for 3 hours.

4. Serve hot, warm, or cold.

Curried Almonds

MAKES 2 TO 3 SERVINGS

The next time someone expresses concern about your protein intake, tell them not to worry; you eat almonds. Just 2 ounces of almonds supplies almost 8 grams of protein (an egg supplies less than 6 grams of protein!). Even if you're craving sweets, almonds can be a great snack. Try brown sugar and cinnamon in place of the curry powder and seasoned salt in this recipe.

2 TABLESPOONS VEGAN MARGARINE, MELTED

1 TABLESPOON CURRY POWDER

½ TEASPOON SEASONED SALT

1 POUND BLANCHED ALMONDS

1. Combine the vegan margarine, curry powder, and seasoned salt in the slow cooker.

2. Stir in the almonds.

3. Cover and cook on low for 2 to 3 hours.

4. Turn the slow cooker to high, remove the cover, and cook for 1 to 1½ hours more.

5. Serve warm or at room temperature.

Spicy Pecans

The pecan's rich, buttery flavor is enhanced by the blend of spices and powdered sugar in this snack recipe. These nuts are North American natives, and the United States produces most of the world's pecans. If pecans are not to your liking, substitute walnuts or cashews, or any combination of your favorite nuts.

1 POUND PECANS
½ CUP VEGAN MARGARINE, MELTED
½ CUP POWDERED SUGAR
1½ TEASPOONS GROUND CINNAMON
½ TEASPOON GROUND GINGER
½ TEASPOON GROUND CARDAMOM
¼ TEASPOON GROUND NUTMEG
⅛ TEASPOON GROUND CLOVES

1. Preheat the slow cooker on high for 15 minutes.

2. Add the pecans, vegan margarine, and powdered sugar to the preheated slow cooker.

3. Stir to coat the pecans evenly.

4. Cover and cook on high for 15 minutes.

5. Reduce the heat to low, remove the lid, and cook for an additional 2 hours, or until the pecans are coated with a crisp glaze.

6. Transfer the pecans to a large bowl.

7. In a small bowl, combine the cinnamon, ginger, cardamom, nutmeg, and cloves.

8. Sift the spices over the pecans.

9. Stir the pecans to distribute the spices evenly.

10. Cool the pecans before serving.

Nutty Coconut Curry Mix

MAKES 4 SERVINGS

It's easy to eat too much of this tasty snack. A blend of nuts, spices, and coconut, it's good for you but a little high in fat. You simply need to practice portion control by storing individual servings in tightly sealed containers.

2 CUPS CRUNCHY RICE CEREAL

1½ CUPS SALTED CASHEWS

1 (5-OUNCE) CAN VEGAN CRISPY CHINESE NOODLES

½ CUP UNSWEETENED FLAKED COCONUT

1 TEASPOON CURRY POWDER

¼ TEASPOON GROUND GINGER

¼ CUP VEGAN MARGARINE, MELTED

1 TABLESPOON SOY SAUCE

1. Combine the rice cereal, cashews, Chinese noodles, and coconut in the slow cooker.

2. Sprinkle the cereal mix with the curry powder and ginger.

3. Add the vegan margarine and soy sauce.

4. Stir all the ingredients together thoroughly.

5. Cover and cook on low for 3 to 4 hours. Remove the lid during the last 30 minutes of cooking.

6. Serve hot or at room temperature.

Root Vegetables with Oil and Vinegar

MAKES 4 SERVINGS

Instead of dressing up your salad with olive oil and balsamic vinegar, how about dressing up your root vegetables? These starchy vegetables are a fantastic source of minerals because they grow underground and absorb myriad nutrients from the soil. Root vegetables can be safely stored for long periods of time and therefore enjoyed throughout the year. Other root vegetables can be substituted for the ones called for here.

4 SHALLOTS, CUT IN HALF

3 LARGE CARROTS, CUT INTO 1-INCH PIECES

2 SMALL TURNIPS, PEELED AND CUT INTO 1-INCH PIECES

1 LARGE PARSNIP, PEELED AND CUT INTO 1-INCH PIECES

2 TABLESPOONS OLIVE OIL

2 TABLESPOONS BALSAMIC VINEGAR

2 TABLESPOONS WATER

1 TABLESPOON PACKED LIGHT BROWN SUGAR

SEA SALT AND CRACKED BLACK PEPPER, TO TASTE

1. Combine the shallots, carrots, turnips, and parsnips in the slow cooker.

2. In a small bowl, combine the olive oil, balsamic vinegar, water, and brown sugar.

3. Pour the mixture over the vegetables in the slow cooker and season with the sea salt and black pepper. Stir to combine.

4. Cover and cook on low for 8 hours, or until the vegetables are soft. Stir once about halfway through, if possible.

5. Serve hot.

Sweet Acorn Squash

Acorn squash, also called pepper squash or Des Moines squash, is easily recognized by its unique longitudinal creases and its dark green color with a splash of orange. Acorn squash's bright orange-yellow flesh is indicative of the squash's beta carotene content. This squash contains abundant dietary fiber and potassium. Acorn squash is inherently sweet, and preparing it in a slow cooker brings out the sweetness even more.

½ CUP APPLE JUICE OR APPLE CIDER

1 LARGE ACORN SQUASH, QUARTERED AND SEEDED

⅛ TEASPOON SEA SALT

¼ CUP DRIED CRANBERRIES

2 TABLESPOONS PACKED LIGHT BROWN SUGAR

2 TABLESPOONS VEGAN MARGARINE

1½ CUPS PEELED, DICED TART APPLES

¼ LEMON

1 TEASPOON GROUND CINNAMON

2 TABLESPOONS MAPLE SYRUP

3 TABLESPOONS WALNUTS (OPTIONAL)

1. Preheat the slow cooker on high for 15 minutes.

2. Pour the apple juice into the preheated slow cooker.

3. Place the squash, cut sides up, in the bottom of the slow cooker.

4. Sprinkle the squash with the sea salt.

5. Top each piece of squash with one-quarter of the dried cranberries, brown sugar, and vegan margarine.

6. Scatter the tart apples on top of and around the squash.

7. Squeeze the lemon over the top of the apples.

continued ▶

8. Sprinkle the apples with the cinnamon.

9. Pour the maple syrup over the top.

10. Cover and cook on low for 4 to 6 hours or on high for 2½ to 4 hours.

11. When the squash is tender, serve hot, sprinkled with the walnuts, if desired.

Stuffed Picante Onions

MAKES 4 SERVINGS

Stuffed onions go well with holiday meals; think mashed potatoes and gravy, fresh green beans, and a vegan loaf. Onions, stuffed or not, are a good part of an anti-inflammatory diet and provide almost 20 percent of your daily vitamin C.

4 MEDIUM WHITE ONIONS, PEELED

2 CUPS CHOPPED BROCCOLI FLORETS

1 CUP DRIED BREAD CRUMBS

2 ROMA TOMATOES, DICED

¼ CUP CHOPPED RED BELL PEPPER

½ TEASPOON DRIED OREGANO

SEA SALT AND CRACKED BLACK PEPPER, TO TASTE

4 TABLESPOONS VEGAN MARGARINE

CAYENNE PEPPER, TO TASTE

½ CUP WATER

1. Hollow out the white onions, creating a cavity in the center but leaving the bottom intact.

2. In a large bowl, combine the broccoli, bread crumbs, tomatoes, bell pepper, oregano, sea salt, and black pepper.

3. Fill the onions with the broccoli mixture.

4. Top each onion with 1 tablespoon of the vegan margarine.

5. Sprinkle each onion with cayenne pepper.

6. Place the stuffed onions in the slow cooker.

7. Pour the water around the stuffed onions, not over them.

8. Cook on low for 6 to 8 hours, or until the onions are tender.

9. Serve hot.

Sweet Potato Casserole

MAKES 6 TO 8 SERVINGS

The sweet potato is a starchy root vegetable, making it an excellent source of the carbohydrates needed to fuel the body and the brain and to sustain energy levels. A staple food in many parts of the world, sweet potatoes are a pleasant alternative to the white potato. When serving this casserole, add some vegan mini marshmallows in place of or in addition to the pecan topping. Melt the marshmallows during the last few minutes of cooking time to increase the sweetness of this dish.

NONSTICK COOKING SPRAY

2 (18-OUNCE) CANS SWEET POTATOES, DRAINED AND MASHED

⅓ CUP PLUS 2 TABLESPOONS VEGAN MARGARINE, MELTED

2 TABLESPOONS GRANULATED SUGAR

2 TABLESPOONS PLUS ⅓ CUP PACKED LIGHT BROWN SUGAR

EGG SUBSTITUTE EQUIVALENT TO 2 EGGS

½ CUP UNSWEETENED SOY MILK

1 TABLESPOON FRESH ORANGE JUICE

⅓ CUP CHOPPED PECANS

2 TABLESPOONS ALL-PURPOSE FLOUR

1. Lightly spray the slow cooker with the nonstick cooking spray.

2. Combine the sweet potatoes, ⅓ cup of the vegan margarine, the granulated sugar, and 2 tablespoons of the brown sugar in the slow cooker.

3. Stir in the egg substitute, soy milk, and fresh orange juice.

4. In a medium bowl, combine the pecans, flour, remaining ⅓ cup brown sugar, and remaining 2 tablespoons vegan margarine.

5. Spread the pecan mixture over the sweet potatoes in the slow cooker.

6. Cover and cook on high for 3 to 4 hours.

7. Serve hot.

Mashed Cauliflower and Garlic "Potatoes"

MAKES 4 TO 6 SERVINGS

This recipe is a great alternative to classic mashed potatoes. Using cauliflower instead means a lot fewer calories and a distinctly different taste. Serve as you would any other mashed potato dish. Chives and green onions, anyone?

1 LARGE HEAD CAULIFLOWER, CUT INTO FLORETS

3 CUPS WATER

4 LARGE GARLIC CLOVES, PEELED

1 TEASPOON SEA SALT

1 BAY LEAF

1 TABLESPOON VEGAN MARGARINE

SOY MILK, AS NEEDED

SEA SALT AND CRACKED BLACK PEPPER, TO TASTE

1. Place the cauliflower in the slow cooker.

2. Add the water, garlic cloves, sea salt, and bay leaf.

3. Cover and cook on high for 2 to 3 hours or on low for 4 to 6 hours.

4. Remove the garlic cloves and bay leaf.

5. Drain out the water.

6. Add the vegan margarine and allow it to melt.

7. Use a potato masher or an immersion blender to make the mixture the consistency of mashed potatoes. If needed, add the soy milk 1 tablespoon at a time.

8. Season with sea salt and black pepper.

9. Serve hot.

Tomato Salsa

MAKES 2 TO 4 SERVINGS

Most Mexican restaurants serve chips and salsa before a meal, and so can you.
If you like your salsa a little spicier, leave the seeds in the jalapeño peppers.
Serve with your favorite baked tortilla chips.

10 PLUM TOMATOES, CORED
2 GARLIC CLOVES
1 MEDIUM YELLOW ONION, CUT INTO WEDGES
2 SMALL JALAPEÑO PEPPERS, STEMS AND SEEDS REMOVED
¼ CUP CHOPPED FRESH CILANTRO
½ TEASPOON SEA SALT

1. Cut a small slit in two of the plum tomatoes.

2. Insert a garlic clove into each slit.

3. Combine all the tomatoes, the onion, and the jalapeño peppers in the slow cooker.

4. Cover and cook on high for 2½ to 3 hours, or until vegetables are softened.

5. Remove the tomato mixture from the slow cooker and allow to cool.

6. Combine the tomato mixture, cilantro, and sea salt in a blender or food processor.

7. Blend or process the ingredients until as smooth or as chunky as you like it.

8. Serve at room temperature.

Marinated Mushrooms

MAKES 4 TO 6 SERVINGS

Mushrooms are a great addition to a healthful vegan lifestyle. Typically thought of as vegetables and not the fungi they really are, mushrooms provide dietary fiber, potassium, and selenium. Seek out organic mushrooms, since mushrooms have a tendency to absorb anything they come into contact with. Serve these marinated mushrooms with warm French or Italian bread, lightly brushed with olive oil and accompanied by roasted red peppers for an appetizer your guests will love.

1 CUP SOY SAUCE

1 CUP WATER

½ CUP VEGAN MARGARINE

1 CUP SUGAR

1 POUND ORGANIC MUSHROOMS, STEMS REMOVED

1. In a medium saucepan over low heat, heat the soy sauce, water, and vegan margarine until the margarine melts.

2. Add the sugar to the soy sauce mixture and stir until the sugar is completely dissolved.

3. Place the mushrooms in the slow cooker.

4. Pour the soy sauce mixture over the mushrooms.

5. Cover and cook on low for 8 to 10 hours, stirring once every hour.

6. Chill the mushrooms before serving.

Spiced Indian Chickpeas

MAKES 6 SERVINGS

People who consume chickpeas on a regular basis have been found to experience a lot more satisfaction in their overall diet. No one is sure why; it might have something to do with the legume's high fiber content or nutrient composition. Consumers of chickpeas were also found to eat healthier overall. Maybe this is why chickpeas are the most widely consumed legume on the planet. This appetizer will surely be a big hit at your next dinner party.

2 (15-OUNCE) CANS CHICKPEAS, RINSED AND DRAINED,
    ¾ CUP LIQUID RESERVED
1 (14½-OUNCE) CAN DICED TOMATOES, DRAINED
3 GARLIC CLOVES, MINCED
1 MEDIUM YELLOW ONION, CHOPPED
1 (1-INCH) PIECE FRESH GINGER, PEELED AND GRATED
1 TEASPOON CRACKED BLACK PEPPER
1 TEASPOON GROUND CLOVES
1 TEASPOON GROUND CUMIN
½ TEASPOON GROUND CARDAMOM
½ TEASPOON GROUND CORIANDER
½ TEASPOON SEA SALT
3 DRIED RED CHILES
2 BAY LEAVES
1 CINNAMON STICK
CHOPPED FRESH CILANTRO, FOR GARNISH

1. Combine the chickpeas, reserved chickpea liquid, tomatoes, garlic, onion, and ginger in the slow cooker.

2. Stir in the black pepper, cloves, cumin, cardamom, coriander, salt, chiles, bay leaves, and cinnamon stick.

3. Cover and cook on low for 8 to 9 hours.

4. Remove and discard the chiles, bay leaves, and cinnamon stick.

5. Serve hot, garnished with fresh cilantro.

Nontraditional Antipasto

MAKES 6 SERVINGS

Are you serving Italian tonight? Traditional antipasto (which means "before the meal") is full of a variety of cured meats, cheeses, and even seafood. Those foods aren't welcome here; however, this roasted vegetable antipasto, made with an assortment of vegetables and mushrooms, is. Dressed with olive oil and served on a decorative platter, this meal starter will spark your guests' interest for whatever lies ahead.

3 MEDIUM CARROTS, PEELED AND CUT INTO 3-INCH STRIPS

2 MEDIUM PARSNIPS, PEELED AND CUT INTO 3-INCH STRIPS

2 SMALL TURNIPS, PEELED AND CUT INTO 2-INCH PIECES

24 WHOLE WHITE PEARL ONIONS, PEELED

1 LARGE RED BELL PEPPER, SEEDED AND CUT INTO 3-INCH STRIPS

1 LARGE YELLOW BELL PEPPER, SEEDED AND CUT INTO 3-INCH STRIPS

1 FENNEL BULB, CUT LENGTHWISE INTO 3-INCH-LONG SLICES
(½ INCH THICK)

12 BABY ARTICHOKES, STEMS INTACT BUT PEELED

8 OUNCES LARGE MUSHROOMS, WASHED AND SLICED INTO
¾-INCH PIECES

4 GARLIC CLOVES, MINCED

1 CUP OLIVE OIL

¾ TEASPOON SEA SALT

CRACKED BLACK PEPPER, TO TASTE

1. Combine the carrots, parsnips, turnips, onions, red and yellow bell peppers, fennel, artichokes, and mushrooms in the slow cooker.

2. Sprinkle the vegetables with the garlic and mix thoroughly.

3. Cover and cook on low for 8 to 10 hours or on high for 3 to 4 hours, or until the vegetables are tender.

continued ▶

4. To brown, place the vegetables under the broiler for 3 to 4 minutes on each side, in batches as necessary.

5. Allow the vegetables to reach room temperature before serving.

6. Arrange the vegetables on a serving platter and drizzle with the olive oil.

7. Season the vegetables with the sea salt and black pepper and toss.

8. Serve immediately.

Mexican Bean Dip

MAKES 7 CUPS

This bean dip makes a wonderful prelude to dinner. This combination of kidney beans, black beans, corn, and tomatoes, along with a cascade of seasonings, deserves more than a regular corn chip. Try multigrain chips for added flavor and nutrition, and dig in.

1 (15-OUNCE) CAN KIDNEY BEANS, RINSED AND DRAINED

1 (15-OUNCE) CAN BLACK BEANS, RINSED AND DRAINED

1 (15-OUNCE) CAN WHOLE KERNEL CORN, DRAINED

1 (14 ½-OUNCE) CAN STEWED TOMATOES

1 (8-OUNCE) CAN TOMATO SAUCE

1 (4-OUNCE) CAN CHOPPED GREEN CHILES, DRAINED

1 (1-OUNCE) ENVELOPE VEGAN TACO SEASONING MIX

½ CUP CHOPPED ONION

2 OR 3 GARLIC CLOVES, MINCED

½ TEASPOON GROUND CUMIN

1. Combine the kidney beans, black beans, corn, stewed tomatoes, tomato sauce, green chiles, seasoning mix, onion, garlic, and cumin in the slow cooker.

2. Stir together, mixing well.

3. Cover and cook on low for 5 to 7 hours.

4. Serve warm.

CHAPTER FIVE

Soups

HOT AND SOUR SOUP

GARLICKY TOMATO SOUP

OLD-FASHIONED SPLIT PEA SOUP

A LITTLE MORE THAN
    SPLIT PEA SOUP

CREAMY BUTTERNUT
    SQUASH SOUP

MOM'S VEGETABLE SOUP

ALPHABET MINESTRONE

VEGGIE AND CHICKPEA SOUP

BEAN AND GREENS SOUP

CREAMY CHICKPEA SOUP

COCONUT, SQUASH,
    AND TOFU SOUP

SPLIT MUNG BEAN SOUP

BLACK BEAN SOUP

VEGGIE AND LENTIL SOUP

LENTIL AND MUSHROOM SOUP

PEARL BARLEY AND LENTIL SOUP

MOROCCAN-STYLE LENTIL SOUP

BEANS, BEANS, AND
    MORE BEANS SOUP

BEAN AND PENNE SOUP

JAMAICAN RED BEAN SOUP

CREAMY BAKED POTATO
    AND VEGGIE SOUP

CHAPTER FIVE

Soups

Hot and Sour Soup

Hot and Sour Soup is eaten in many countries in southeast Asia, including China, Vietnam, and Cambodia. Each country has its own version. Many of these versions have a base of meat, poultry, fish, or shrimp, but this vegan version is just as tasty. Serve with warm crusty bread and this soup becomes a meal.

1 CUP DRIED SHIITAKE MUSHROOMS

3½ CUPS HOT WATER

¾ CUP VEGETABLE STOCK (PAGE 20)

1 CUP CUBED FIRM TOFU

12 OUNCES BAMBOO SHOOTS, SLICED INTO STRIPS

1 CUP HALVED BABY CARROTS

4 GARLIC CLOVES, MINCED

2 TABLESPOONS MINCED FRESH GINGER

¼ CUP RICE VINEGAR

¼ CUP SOY SAUCE

3 TEASPOONS ASIAN CHILI SAUCE

SEA SALT AND CRACKED BLACK PEPPER, TO TASTE

3 TABLESPOONS CORNSTARCH DISSOLVED IN ¼ CUP COLD WATER

1. Soak the dried shiitake mushrooms in the hot water for 20 minutes to soften.

2. Combine the vegetable stock, tofu, bamboo shoots, baby carrots, garlic, ginger, rice vinegar, soy sauce, and Asian chili sauce in the slow cooker.

3. Remove the mushrooms from the water and slice into long thin strips.

4. Add the mushrooms to the slow cooker.

5. Season the soup with the sea salt and black pepper.

6. Cover and cook on low for 6 to 8 hours.

7. Stir the cornstarch mixture into the soup to thicken.

8. Cook for an additional 20 to 30 minutes.

9. Stir the soup, ladle it into bowls, and serve hot.

Garlicky Tomato Soup

Are you a garlic lover? If so, welcome aboard. Garlic might not inspire good breath, but it can inspire good health. Garlic is a member of the allium family and contains many sulfur-containing compounds. These compounds are responsible for garlic's many health-promoting benefits, such as protection against cardiovascular disease and cancer, antibacterial and antiviral properties, and improved metabolism of iron.

6 CUPS VEGETABLE STOCK (PAGE 20)
1 (15-OUNCE) CAN TOMATO SOUP
6 GARLIC CLOVES, MINCED
1 TABLESPOON DRIED OREGANO
1 TABLESPOON DRIED THYME
1 TO 2 BAY LEAVES
SEA SALT, TO TASTE
GARLIC BREAD (OPTIONAL)

1. Combine the vegetable stock, tomato soup, garlic, oregano, thyme, bay leaves, and sea salt in the slow cooker and stir well.

2. Cover and cook on low for 6 to 8 hours.

3. Remove the bay leaves.

4. Ladle the soup into bowls and serve hot with the garlic bread, if desired.

Old-Fashioned Split Pea Soup

MAKES 8 SERVINGS

Did you know that split peas are an excellent source of molybdenum? One cup of cooked split peas supplies 196 percent of the daily value of this essential trace element. Molybdenum is not completely understood, but it is necessary for the functioning of certain enzymes. Split peas provide fiber, protein, folate, and myriad other nutrients, too. In addition, this soup is delicious, and enhanced even more by a grilled vegan cheese and tomato sandwich on the side.

18 CUPS VEGETABLE STOCK (PAGE 20)
2 CUPS DRIED SPLIT PEAS
2 LARGE POTATOES, PEELED AND CHOPPED
2 CELERY STALKS, CHOPPED
2 LARGE CARROTS, SLICED
2 BAY LEAVES

1. Combine the vegetable stock, split peas, potatoes, celery, carrots, and bay leaves in the slow cooker.

2. Cover and cook on low for 4 hours, or until the split peas are soft.

3. Remove the bay leaves.

4. Ladle the soup into bowls and serve hot.

A Little More Than Split Pea Soup

MAKES 6 SERVINGS

This split pea soup provides the same nutrient density as Old-Fashioned Split Pea Soup but with added cauliflower and different seasonings. Traditional Dutch accompaniments to split pea soup include pumpernickel bread with bacon or sausage and stone ground mustard. Hmmm . . . the bread and mustard sound good.

6 CUPS VEGETABLE STOCK (PAGE 20)

2 CUPS DRIED SPLIT PEAS

3 CUPS CAULIFLOWER FLORETS, CHOPPED INTO ½-INCH PIECES

1 CELERY STALK, DICED

1 MEDIUM YELLOW ONION, DICED

2 GARLIC CLOVES, MINCED

1 TEASPOON GROUND CUMIN

½ TEASPOON GROUND SAGE

½ TEASPOON GROUND THYME

1 BAY LEAF

SEA SALT AND CRACKED BLACK PEPPER, TO TASTE

OLIVE OIL (OPTIONAL)

1. Combine the vegetable stock, split peas, cauliflower, celery, onion, garlic, cumin, sage, thyme, and bay leaf in the slow cooker.

2. Cook on low for 8 hours, or until the split peas are soft.

3. Remove the bay leaf.

4. Season with the sea salt and the black pepper.

5. Ladle the soup into bowls, drizzle with the olive oil (if desired), and serve hot.

Creamy Butternut Squash Soup

Butternut squash is never better than when it is puréed and creamy. There's no dairy, just wholesome food made better with help from your immersion blender. Dunking bread in this soup is encouraged.

1 SMALL BUTTERNUT SQUASH, SEEDED, PEELED, AND CUT
    INTO 2-INCH CUBES
2 GARLIC CLOVES, CRUSHED
1 CUP WATER
3 CUPS VEGETABLE STOCK (PAGE 20)
1 LARGE YELLOW ONION, CHOPPED
1 TABLESPOON GRATED FRESH GINGER
1 TEASPOON SUGAR
1 TEASPOON SEA SALT
¼ TEASPOON CRACKED BLACK PEPPER
WARM CRUSTY BREAD (OPTIONAL)

1. Place the squash cubes and garlic in the slow cooker with ¼ cup of the water.

2. Cover and cook on low for 5 hours or on high for 3 hours, or until the squash is tender.

3. Remove the squash from the slow cooker.

4. Discard the garlic and the remaining liquid in the slow cooker.

5. Return the squash to the slow cooker.

6. Add the vegetable stock, onion, ginger, sugar, and remaining ¾ cup water to the slow cooker.

continued ▶

7. Purée the soup using the handheld immersion blender. Keep the blender's head below the soup's surface and purée until completely smooth.

8. Season with the sea salt and black pepper and stir.

9. Cover and cook the soup for an additional 30 minutes.

10. Serve hot with warm crusty bread, if desired.

Mom's Vegetable Soup

MAKES 4 TO 6 SERVINGS

Remember coming in out of the cold after trudging home from school on a bleak winter day? Remember your mom standing in the doorway, a hot drink in one hand and a warm cup of soup in the other? This is that soup. It's so good it fills you not only with warmth and nutrients, but with comfort from an earlier time, too.

2 MEDIUM CARROTS, CHOPPED

1 MEDIUM YELLOW ONION, CHOPPED

1 CELERY STALK, CHOPPED

1 TABLESPOON OLIVE OIL

6 CUPS VEGETABLE STOCK (PAGE 20)

2 SMALL RED POTATOES, DICED

½ LARGE RED BELL PEPPER, SEEDED AND CHOPPED

4 OUNCES GREEN BEANS, CUT INTO 1-INCH PIECES

1 LARGE GARLIC CLOVE, MINCED

1 (15-OUNCE) CAN WHITE BEANS, RINSED AND DRAINED

½ CUP FROZEN PEAS

SEA SALT AND CRACKED BLACK PEPPER, TO TASTE

2 TABLESPOONS CHOPPED FRESH PARSLEY

WHOLE-GRAIN CRACKERS (OPTIONAL)

1. Combine the carrots, onion, celery, and olive oil in the slow cooker.

2. Cover and cook on high for 4 to 6 hours.

3. Stir in the vegetable stock, potatoes, bell pepper, green beans, and garlic.

4. Turn the slow cooker to low, cover, and cook for 8 hours.

5. About 30 minutes prior to serving, stir in the white beans and peas.

6. Season with sea salt and black pepper.

continued ▶

7. Add the fresh parsley immediately before serving.

8. Ladle the soup into bowls and serve hot with whole-grain crackers, if desired.

Alphabet Minestrone

MAKES 8 SERVINGS

Alphabet minestrone is a clever and fun way to get kids to eat their veggies. All the coaxing and pleading are unnecessary when those veggies are presented in a soup bowl. The alphabet macaroni is a bit of added fun and a motivator for the young ones. Make it a game and watch the soup disappear.

6 CUPS VEGETABLE STOCK (PAGE 20)

1 (28-OUNCE) CAN CRUSHED TOMATOES

1 (15-OUNCE) CAN KIDNEY BEANS, RINSED AND DRAINED

1 CUP HALVED GREEN BEANS

1 LARGE YELLOW ONION, CHOPPED

2 LARGE CARROTS, DICED

2 CELERY STALKS, DICED

1 SMALL ZUCCHINI, DICED

3 GARLIC CLOVES, MINCED

1 TABLESPOON MINCED FRESH PARSLEY

1½ TEASPOONS DRIED OREGANO

1 TEASPOON SEA SALT

¾ TEASPOON DRIED THYME

¼ TEASPOON CRACKED BLACK PEPPER

½ CUP COOKED ALPHABET MACARONI

4 CUPS CHOPPED FRESH SPINACH

FINELY GRATED VEGAN PARMESAN CHEESE (OPTIONAL)

FAVORITE BREAD OR CRACKERS (OPTIONAL)

1. Combine the vegetable stock, crushed tomatoes, kidney beans, green beans, onion, carrots, celery, and zucchini in the slow cooker.

2. Stir in the garlic, parsley, oregano, sea salt, thyme, and black pepper.

3. Cover and cook on low for 6 to 8 hours.

4. Add the alphabet macaroni and the spinach to the minestrone.

continued ▶

5. Cover and cook for an additional 15 minutes.

6. Ladle the soup into bowls, top with the vegan Parmesan cheese (if desired), and serve hot with your favorite bread or crackers.

Veggie and Chickpea Soup

MAKES 8 SERVINGS

Chickpeas provide a strong foundation for this veggie soup. Chickpeas have been grown for thousands of years in the Middle East. Today, India is the number one producer of chickpeas; they are also produced in the United States.

4 CUPS VEGETABLE STOCK (PAGE 20)

2 (15-OUNCE) CANS CHICKPEAS, RINSED AND DRAINED

2 CUPS DICED ZUCCHINI

1 CUP PEELED AND DICED CARROTS

1 CUP SLICED GREEN BEANS

2 CELERY STALKS, DICED

¼ CUP TOMATO PASTE

2 TABLESPOONS OLIVE OIL

1 TABLESPOON SOY SAUCE

1 TEASPOON DRIED THYME

1 TEASPOON GROUND PAPRIKA

1 TEASPOON GROUND CORIANDER

½ TEASPOON GROUND FENNEL

¼ TEASPOON GROUND GINGER

¼ TEASPOON GARLIC POWDER

1 (2-INCH) PIECE DRIED KOMBU SEAWEED, RINSED

1 BAY LEAF

½ CUP COARSELY CHOPPED FRESH BASIL

SEA SALT AND CRACKED BLACK PEPPER, TO TASTE

PITA BREAD, QUARTERED, HEATED, AND LIGHTLY SPRINKLED WITH
     GARLIC SALT (OPTIONAL)

1. Combine the vegetable stock, chickpeas, zucchini, carrots, green beans, celery, tomato paste, olive oil, and soy sauce in the slow cooker.

2. Stir in the thyme, paprika, coriander, fennel, ginger, garlic powder, seaweed, and bay leaf.

continued ▶

3. Cover and cook on low for 4 to 6 hours.

4. Remove the seaweed and the bay leaf.

5. Add the fresh basil, sea salt, and black pepper.

6. Ladle the soup into bowls and serve hot with the pita bread, if desired.

Bean and Greens Soup

The great thing about beans and greens is that you can use any type of bean or any type of green you fancy. This soup showcases cannellini beans and kale. Cannellini beans are sometimes referred to as white kidney beans. Popular in Italian cooking, these beans are high in fiber and protein and low in fat. Kale is a green that comes highly recommended in terms of its nutrient density and is rivaled only by collard greens.

NONSTICK COOKING SPRAY

4 TO 5 CUPS VEGETABLE STOCK (PAGE 20)

2 (15-OUNCE) CANS CANNELLINI BEANS, RINSED, DRAINED, AND PURÉED

1 (14½-OUNCE) CAN DICED TOMATOES, UNDRAINED

2 MEDIUM YELLOW ONIONS, DICED

2 TABLESPOONS MINCED GARLIC

2 TEASPOONS DRIED ITALIAN SEASONING

½ TEASPOON DRIED RUBBED SAGE

8 OUNCES KALE, STEMMED AND FINELY CHOPPED

GRATED VEGAN PARMESAN CHEESE (OPTIONAL)

1. Lightly spray the slow cooker with the nonstick cooking spray.

2. Pour the vegetable stock into the slow cooker.

3. Stir in the puréed beans, tomatoes with their juices, onions, garlic, Italian seasoning, and sage.

4. Cover and cook for 8 to 10 hours on low or 4 hours on high.

5. Add the kale to the slow cooker during the last 2 hours of the cooking process.

6. Ladle the soup into bowls, top with the vegan Parmesan cheese (if desired), and serve hot.

Creamy Chickpea Soup

MAKES 8 SERVINGS

A nondairy approach to a creamy soup is a win-win for everyone. Dairy is not an option in a vegan diet and, really, who needs it? Dairy is full of saturated fat and cholesterol, while chickpeas are a healthful and cruelty-free way to thicken pretty much anything. Hummus is a great example, and so is this soup.

4 CUPS VEGETABLE STOCK (PAGE 20)

2 (15-OUNCE) CANS CHICKPEAS, RINSED AND DRAINED

1 (28-OUNCE) CAN CRUSHED TOMATOES

2 LARGE CARROTS, CHOPPED

2 CELERY STALKS, DICED

2 GARLIC CLOVES, MINCED

2 TABLESPOONS OLIVE OIL

2 TABLESPOONS TOMATO PASTE

1 TABLESPOON DRIED BASIL

1 TABLESPOON SUGAR

1 TABLESPOON SOY SAUCE

1 TEASPOON GROUND CUMIN

1 TEASPOON SMOKED PAPRIKA

½ TEASPOON SEA SALT

1 PINCH CHIPOTLE PEPPER POWDER

2 BAY LEAVES

SHREDDED VEGAN MOZZARELLA CHEESE (OPTIONAL)

CHOPPED FRESH PARSLEY (OPTIONAL)

ARTISANAL BREAD (OPTIONAL)

1. Combine the vegetable stock, chickpeas, tomatoes, carrots, celery, garlic, olive oil, tomato paste, basil, sugar, soy sauce, cumin, paprika, sea salt, chipotle pepper powder, and bay leaves in the slow cooker and stir well.

2. Cover and cook on low for 5 hours.

3. Remove the bay leaves.

4. Purée the soup using a handheld immersion blender. Keep the blender's head below the soup's surface and purée as little or as much as desired.

5. Ladle the soup into bowls, top with the shredded vegan mozzarella cheese and fresh parsley (if using), and serve hot with artisanal bread, if desired.

Coconut, Squash, and Tofu Soup

MAKES 6 SERVINGS

To accompany this delightful soup, make some Slow-Cooked Brown Basmati Rice (page 22) ahead of time or use two slow cookers at once. Including tofu in this soup will help you develop your tofu-pressing skills.

1 LARGE BUTTERNUT SQUASH, COOKED AND PURÉED

2 CELERY STALKS, CHOPPED

2 MEDIUM CARROTS, DICED

1 STALK LEMON GRASS, PEELED AND CUT INTO 2-INCH PIECES

1 TEASPOON SUNFLOWER OIL

1 TEASPOON GROUND GINGER

½ TEASPOON GROUND CUMIN

½ TEASPOON GROUND TURMERIC

½ TEASPOON SEA SALT

⅛ TEASPOON CAYENNE PEPPER, OR TO TASTE

1 (14-OUNCE) CAN LIGHT COCONUT MILK

½ POUND FIRM TOFU, DRAINED AND PRESSED (PAGE 14)

CHOPPED FRESH CILANTRO, FOR GARNISH

1. Combine the butternut squash, celery, carrots, lemon grass, sunflower oil, ginger, cumin, turmeric, sea salt, cayenne pepper, and coconut milk in the slow cooker and stir well.

2. Cover and cook on low for 2 hours.

3. Add the tofu and turn the slow cooker to high. Cover and cook for an additional 15 to 20 minutes.

4. Ladle the soup into bowls, garnish with the fresh cilantro, and serve hot.

Split Mung Bean Soup

You may have never have heard of split mung beans; they are much more common in Indian cuisine than in American cuisine. Mung beans are yellow lentils, and when combined with the Indian spices in this recipe, they form what is known as a mung dal, or Indian-flavored yellow lentil soup. Precook the spices in order to bring out the flavor of this hearty soup.

½ CUP SPLIT MUNG BEANS

3 CUPS VEGETABLE STOCK (PAGE 20)

1 SMALL YAM, PEELED AND CUT INTO 1-INCH PIECES

1 CELERY STALK, THINLY SLICED

1 BAY LEAF

1 TO 2 TABLESPOONS OLIVE OIL

1 TEASPOON GROUND CORIANDER

½ TEASPOON GROUND CUMIN

½ TEASPOON GROUND GINGER

½ TEASPOON GROUND FENNEL

¼ TEASPOON GROUND TURMERIC

PINCH OF CAYENNE PEPPER

CRACKED BLACK PEPPER, TO TASTE

2 CUPS CHOPPED FRESH SPINACH

1 TABLESPOON FRESH LEMON JUICE

½ TEASPOON SEA SALT

CHOPPED FRESH CILANTRO, FOR GARNISH

CHAPATI (OPTIONAL)

1. Rinse the split mung beans and soak in water for 1 hour.

2. Drain the split mung beans and put them in the slow cooker.

3. Add the vegetable stock, yam, celery, and bay leaf.

4. Cover and cook on low for 6 hours.

continued ▶

5. Remove the bay leaf.

6. Turn the slow cooker to high.

7. In a small skillet, warm up the olive oil over low heat.

8. Add the coriander, cumin, ginger, fennel, turmeric, cayenne pepper, and black pepper to the skillet and heat until the seasonings start to bubble.

9. Stir 1 cup of liquid from the slow cooker into the skillet mixture.

10. Transfer the contents of the skillet to the slow cooker.

11. Stir in the spinach, lemon juice, and sea salt.

12. Cover and cook for 5 to 10 minutes.

13. Ladle the soup into bowls, garnish with the fresh cilantro, and serve hot with a side of chapatti, if desired.

Black Bean Soup

A soup-and-sandwich combo is always a crowd pleaser. Start with this tasty, slightly spicy black bean soup, topped with a dollop of vegan sour cream and a sprig of fresh cilantro. Next, cook up a warm grilled cheese sandwich (made with vegan cheese and margarine) in your nonstick skillet and you're on your way.

2 (15-OUNCE) CANS BLACK BEANS, RINSED AND DRAINED

1 (14½-OUNCE) CAN DICED TOMATOES, UNDRAINED

1½ CUPS VEGETABLE STOCK (PAGE 20)

3 GARLIC CLOVES, MINCED

1 JALAPEÑO PEPPER, SEEDED AND DICED

½ GREEN BELL PEPPER, SEEDED AND DICED

¼ LARGE RED ONION, DICED

1½ TABLESPOONS RED WINE VINEGAR

¾ TABLESPOON CHILI POWDER

1 TEASPOON GROUND CUMIN

½ TEASPOON SEA SALT

¼ TEASPOON CRACKED BLACK PEPPER

¼ TEASPOON DRIED OREGANO

⅛ TEASPOON DRIED THYME

1 BAY LEAF

1. Combine the black beans, tomatoes with their juices, vegetable stock, garlic, jalapeño pepper, bell pepper, onion, red wine vinegar, chili powder, cumin, sea salt, black pepper, oregano, thyme, and bay leaf in the slow cooker and stir well.

2. Cover and cook on high for 8 hours.

3. Remove the bay leaf and stir again.

4. Ladle the soup into bowls and serve hot.

Veggie and Lentil Soup

MAKES 4 TO 6 SERVINGS

Veggies and lentils are a healthful combination and just what the doctor might order on a cold winter day. This soup is full of antioxidants, dietary fiber, and L-arginine, an amino acid and precursor to nitric oxide in the body. Nitric oxide is essential for cardiovascular health because it dilates the blood vessels and strengthens the endothelium (the innermost lining of the blood vessels), leading to increased blood flow and better circulation.

2 CUPS DRIED LENTILS, RINSED

4 CUPS WATER

4 CUPS VEGETABLE STOCK (PAGE 20)

1 (14½-OUNCE) CAN DICED TOMATOES, DRAINED

1 MEDIUM YELLOW ONION, DICED

3 CELERY STALKS, SLICED

2 LARGE CARROTS, CHOPPED

2 GARLIC CLOVES, MINCED

1 TEASPOON SEA SALT

½ TEASPOON DRIED OREGANO

¼ TEASPOON CRACKED BLACK PEPPER

LIGHTLY TOASTED PITA BREAD, QUARTERED (OPTIONAL)

1. Combine the lentils, water, and vegetable stock in the slow cooker.

2. Stir in the tomatoes, onion, celery, carrots, garlic, sea salt, oregano, and black pepper.

3. Cover and cook on low for 8 to 10 hours.

4. Stir the soup, ladle it into bowls, and serve hot with toasted pita bread, if desired.

Lentil and Mushroom Soup

MAKES 8 SERVINGS

Dried wild mushrooms give this soup an edge thanks to their highly concentrated flavor. Rehydrating them increases their volume dramatically and creates a tasty broth at the same time. For this recipe you can use any type of dried wild mushrooms: porcinis, shiitakes, chanterelles, or morels, or a mixture.

2 CUPS HOT WATER

2 TABLESPOONS DRIED WILD MUSHROOMS

4 CUPS VEGETABLE STOCK (PAGE 20)

1 (28-OUNCE) CAN DICED TOMATOES, UNDRAINED

2 CUPS DRIED LENTILS, RINSED

1 MEDIUM YELLOW ONION, CHOPPED

4 CELERY STALKS, DICED

2 LARGE CARROTS, PEELED AND DICED

1 TEASPOON CHILI POWDER

2 TABLESPOONS FRESH LEMON JUICE

SEA SALT AND CRACKED BLACK PEPPER, TO TASTE

CHOPPED FRESH CHIVES, FOR GARNISH

1. In a large heatproof bowl combine the hot water and wild mushrooms. Soak the mushrooms for 30 minutes.

2. Strain the mushrooms and reserve the liquid. Pat dry and chop.

3. Combine the mushrooms, reserved soaking liquid, vegetable stock, tomatoes with their juices, lentils, onion, celery, carrots, and chili powder in the slow cooker and stir well.

4. Cover and cook on low for 8 to 10 hours or on high for 4 to 5 hours, or until vegetables are tender.

5. Stir in the lemon juice, sea salt, and black pepper.

6. Ladle the soup into bowls, garnish with the fresh chives, and serve hot.

Pearl Barley and Lentil Soup

MAKES 6 SERVINGS

Pearl barley is not a whole grain; however, it cooks faster than whole-grain barley and is still one step above a refined grain. Refined grains contain no bran and therefore no fiber. Pearl barley may still contain some of its original bran and, unlike other grains, barley's fiber runs through the entire kernel, not just the bran's outer layer. The lentils and vegetables in this soup more than make up for any fiber that may be lacking in the barley.

½ CUP DRIED LENTILS, RINSED

3 TABLESPOONS PEARL BARLEY

½ CUP CHOPPED CARROT

½ CUP CHOPPED CELERY

½ CUP CHOPPED YELLOW ONION

1 GARLIC CLOVE, MINCED

¼ TEASPOON DRIED BASIL

¼ TEASPOON DRIED OREGANO

⅛ TEASPOON DRIED THYME

1 BAY LEAF

1¾ CUPS VEGETABLE STOCK (PAGE 20)

1¼ CUPS WATER

1 (14½-OUNCE) CAN STEWED TOMATOES

2 TABLESPOONS CHOPPED FRESH PARSLEY

1 TABLESPOON APPLE CIDER VINEGAR

WARMED CRUSTY BREAD (OPTIONAL)

1. Combine the lentils, barley, carrot, celery, yellow onion, garlic, basil, oregano, thyme, and bay leaf in the slow cooker.

2. Pour in the vegetable stock, water, and stewed tomatoes and stir.

3. Cover and cook on low for 12 to 14 hours or on high for 5 to 6 hours.

4. Remove the bay leaf.

5. Stir in the parsley and apple cider vinegar.

6. Ladle the soup into bowls and serve hot with the warmed crusty bread, if desired.

Moroccan-Style Lentil Soup

Moroccan cuisine shares many similarities with Indian cuisine, as demonstrated in this Moroccan-style soup. Both cuisines use chickpeas and garam masala, a blend of ground spices. Whether you call them Moroccan or Indian, the flavors in this lentil soup really come together when you use a handheld immersion blender to create a smooth texture. Add a little more heat with a sprinkle of cayenne pepper as a garnish.

4 CUPS VEGETABLE STOCK (PAGE 20)

1 (28-OUNCE) CAN DICED TOMATOES, UNDRAINED

1 (15-OUNCE) CAN CHICKPEAS, RINSED AND DRAINED

1 (15-OUNCE) CAN PINTO BEANS, RINSED AND DRAINED

1 CUP DRIED LENTILS, RINSED

½ CUP CHOPPED CELERY

½ CUP CHOPPED CARROT

1 MEDIUM YELLOW ONION, CHOPPED

2 GARLIC CLOVES, CHOPPED

1 (1-INCH) PIECE FRESH GINGER, PEELED AND MINCED

1½ TEASPOONS GARAM MASALA

½ TEASPOON CAYENNE PEPPER, PLUS MORE FOR GARNISH (OPTIONAL)

½ TEASPOON GROUND CUMIN

¼ TEASPOON GROUND NUTMEG

¼ TEASPOON GROUND CINNAMON

1. Combine the vegetable stock, tomatoes with their juices, chickpeas, pinto beans, lentils, celery, carrots, yellow onion, garlic, and ginger in the slow cooker.

2. Stir in the garam masala, cayenne pepper, cumin, nutmeg, and cinnamon.

3. Cover and cook on low for 8 to 10 hours.

4. Purée the soup using a handheld immersion blender. Keep the blender's head below the soup's surface and purée as little or as much as desired.

5. Ladle the soup into bowls, garnish with additional cayenne pepper (if desired), and serve hot.

Beans, Beans, and More Beans Soup

MAKES 16 SERVINGS

Thirteen kinds of beans? That's a lot! This hearty soup contains a variety of beans, including green split peas, yellow split peas, barley, and lentils. Imagine the protein you'll be getting in this meal. Add a green salad and some bread, and you have dinner.

8 CUPS VEGETABLE STOCK (PAGE 20)
2 (14½-OUNCE) CANS DICED TOMATOES, UNDRAINED
1 (29-OUNCE) BAG 13-BEAN SOUP MIX, RINSED
2 CUPS FROZEN CORN
1 LARGE YELLOW ONION, CHOPPED
3 CELERY STALKS, CHOPPED
3 GARLIC CLOVES, MINCED
1 TABLESPOON DRIED THYME
½ TEASPOON SEA SALT
½ TEASPOON CRACKED BLACK PEPPER
½ TEASPOON RED PEPPER FLAKES

1. Combine the vegetable stock, tomatoes with their juices, bean soup mix, corn, onion, celery, and garlic in the slow cooker.

2. Stir in the thyme, sea salt, black pepper, and red pepper flakes.

3. Cover and cook on low for 8 hours or on high for 4 hours.

4. Ladle the soup into bowls and serve hot.

Bean and Penne Soup

Penne, typically served with sauce and bread, is a welcome addition to soup. A combination of Italian and Indian spices come together to bring a plethora of flavors to your palate. Top it off by adding fresh basil and some shredded vegan mozzarella cheese, and this soup is a nice complement to any dinner.

4 CUPS VEGETABLE STOCK (PAGE 20)

1 CUP COOKED OR CANNED KIDNEY BEANS, RINSED AND DRAINED

1 (8-OUNCE) CAN TOMATO SAUCE

1 MEDIUM CARROT, PEELED AND THINLY SLICED

2 CELERY STALKS, THINLY SLICED

1 MEDIUM POTATO, PEELED AND CUT INTO 1-INCH CUBES

½ RED BELL PEPPER, SEEDED AND CHOPPED

1 JALAPEÑO PEPPER, SEEDED AND MINCED

¼ CUP DICED YELLOW ONION

1 TABLESPOON OLIVE OIL

1 TABLESPOON MINCED FRESH GARLIC

1 TEASPOON DRIED MARJORAM

1 TEASPOON GROUND CORIANDER

1 TEASPOON DRIED BASIL

½ TEASPOON DRIED OREGANO

½ TEASPOON GROUND CUMIN

½ TEASPOON DRIED THYME

⅛ TEASPOON CAYENNE PEPPER

1 CUP PENNE PASTA, COOKED AL DENTE AND RINSED WITH COLD WATER

1 CUP FROZEN GREEN BEANS

½ TEASPOON SEA SALT

1. Combine the vegetable stock , kidney beans, tomato sauce, carrot, celery, potato, bell pepper, jalapeño pepper, onion, olive oil, garlic, marjoram, coriander, basil, oregano, cumin, thyme, and cayenne pepper in the slow cooker and stir well.

continued ▶

2. Cover and cook on low for 4 to 6 hours, or until the veggies are tender.

3. Add the cooked penne, frozen green beans, and sea salt.

4. Turn the heat to high, cover, and cook for an additional 20 minutes or until the pasta and green beans are heated through.

5. Ladle the soup into bowls and serve hot.

Jamaican Red Bean Soup

MAKES 6 SERVINGS

Red kidney beans, coconut milk, thyme, garlic, and yams are popular foods in Jamaican cuisine. Serve this soup with Slow-Cooked Brown Basmati Rice (page 22) and some hard bread for a satisfying Jamaican meal.

1 TABLESPOON OLIVE OIL

2 GARLIC CLOVES, MINCED

2 CUPS SLICED BABY CARROTS

1 (14½-OUNCE) CAN DICED TOMATOES, DRAINED

3 SCALLIONS, CHOPPED

1 SWEET POTATO, PEELED AND DICED

2 TEASPOONS CURRY POWDER

½ TEASPOON DRIED THYME

¼ TEASPOON RED PEPPER FLAKES

¼ TEASPOON GROUND ALLSPICE

SEA SALT AND CRACKED BLACK PEPPER, TO TASTE

2 (15-OUNCE) CANS DARK RED KIDNEY BEANS, RINSED AND DRAINED

1 CUP LIGHT COCONUT MILK

1 TO 2 CUPS VEGETABLE STOCK (PAGE 20)

1. Add the olive oil and the garlic to the slow cooker.

2. Turn the slow cooker to high.

3. Add the carrots, tomatoes, scallions, and sweet potato.

4. Stir in the curry powder, thyme, red pepper flakes, allspice, sea salt, and black pepper.

5. Add the kidney beans, coconut milk, and vegetable stock.

6. Cover and cook on low for 6 to 8 hours.

7. Ladle the soup into bowls and serve hot.

Creamy Baked Potato and Veggie Soup

MAKES 8 SERVINGS

This soup is a vegan spin on an old classic. Texture is everything here, just as with a good mashed potato. Are you a fan of smooth or chunky? Mash the potatoes to your desired consistency for the creamiest, cheesiest baked potato soup ever. It is simply delicious, no matter how you choose to eat it.

3 CUPS VEGETABLE STOCK (PAGE 20)

5 MEDIUM RUSSET POTATOES, PARTIALLY PEELED, CHOPPED INTO ½-INCH CUBES

½ CUP FINELY DICED CELERY

1 SMALL WHITE ONION, DICED

3 GARLIC CLOVES, MINCED

¼ CUP VEGAN MARGARINE

1 TEASPOON SEA SALT

¼ TEASPOON RED PEPPER FLAKES

¼ TEASPOON DRIED DILL

¼ TEASPOON GARLIC POWDER

CRACKED BLACK PEPPER, TO TASTE

½ CUP GRATED VEGAN PARMESAN CHEESE

½ CUP GRATED VEGAN SHARP CHEDDAR CHEESE

CHOPPED SCALLIONS, FOR GARNISH

1. Combine the vegetable stock, potatoes, celery, white onion, garlic, and vegan margarine in the slow cooker.

2. Stir in the salt, red pepper flakes, dill, garlic powder, and black pepper.

3. Cover and cook on low for 8 hours or on high for 4 hours.

4. Stir in the Parmesan cheese and cheddar cheese at the end of the cooking process.

5. Ladle the soup into bowls, garnish with the scallions, and serve hot.

CHAPTER SIX

Stews and Chilies

FROZEN VEGGIE STEW

EASY MILLET STEW

SWEET AND SPICY CHICKPEA STEW

CREAMY CURRY STEW

CREAMY PUMPKIN STEW

VEGGIE AND SQUASH STEW

BLACK BEAN AND CHIPOTLE
   PEPPER STEW

LENTIL AND BEAN STEW

MEXICAN-STYLE DUMPLING STEW

"MEATY" SHIITAKE STEW

TWO-BEAN CHILI

BLACK BEAN AND TOMATO CHILI

BLACK-EYED PEA CHILI

BAKED BEAN CHILI

LIMA BEAN CHILI

SPICY VEGAN CHILI

SWEET POTATO CHILI

QUINOA CHILI

SPICY PUMPKIN CHILI

GREAT NORTHERN BEAN
   "CHICKEN" CHILI

Stews and Chilies

Frozen Veggie Stew

MAKES 4 SERVINGS

This stew uses both fresh and frozen veggies. Depending on when and where you buy your veggies, frozen can be a better choice. Fresh produce is often transported halfway across the country and takes days to arrive on your grocer's shelf, losing nutrients the whole time. Veggies you find in the freezer section of your local grocery are picked and frozen immediately, a process that preserves their nutrients. Buy local fresh produce whenever possible; when you can't, frozen veggies are a great option.

2 CUPS WATER

1½ CUPS VEGETABLE STOCK (PAGE 20)

2 MEDIUM POTATOES, PEELED AND DICED

2 MEDIUM CARROTS, DICED

1 CELERY STALK, DICED

½ MEDIUM YELLOW ONION, MINCED

1 GARLIC CLOVE, MINCED

¼ CUP FROZEN PEAS

¼ CUP FROZEN CORN

¼ CUP HALVED FROZEN GREEN BEANS

¼ CUP SLICED MUSHROOMS

1½ TEASPOONS CHOPPED FRESH PARSLEY

1 BAY LEAF

SEA SALT AND CRACKED BLACK PEPPER, TO TASTE

1 TABLESPOON CORNSTARCH DISSOLVED IN 2 TABLESPOONS COLD
    WATER (OPTIONAL)

CORNBREAD (OPTIONAL)

1. Pour the water and vegetable stock into the slow cooker.

2. Stir in the potatoes, carrots, celery, onion, garlic, peas, corn, green beans, mushrooms, parsley, and bay leaf.

3. Cover and cook on low for 8 to 10 hours.

continued ▶

4. Remove the bay leaf.

5. Season with the sea salt and black pepper.

6. Thicken the stew with the cornstarch mixture if a thicker consistency is desired.

7. Ladle the stew into bowls and serve hot with the cornbread, if desired.

Easy Millet Stew

If you've never tried millet, now's your chance. Millet, the highlight of this simple stew, is classified as an alternative grain because it's gluten-free, but its nutty flavor can certainly be enjoyed by everyone. Millet has been a staple for many cultures across the globe for centuries. It provides health-protective properties and is also a good source of manganese, tryptophan, magnesium, and phosphorus. When served with fruit, millet's flavor is really enhanced.

1 CUP UNCOOKED MILLET

4 CUPS VEGETABLE STOCK (PAGE 20)

2 MEDIUM YELLOW ONIONS, CHOPPED

2 MEDIUM WHITE POTATOES, PEELED AND CUT INTO BITE-SIZE PIECES

2 MEDIUM CARROTS, CHOPPED

2 CELERY STALKS WITH LEAVES, CHOPPED

½ POUND WHITE MUSHROOMS, CHOPPED

½ TEASPOON DRIED BASIL

½ TEASPOON DRIED THYME

2 BAY LEAVES

1 (15-OUNCE) CAN DICED PINEAPPLE, DRAINED (OPTIONAL)

1. Toast the millet in a dry skillet for about 5 minutes, stirring constantly to avoid burning.

2. Transfer the millet to the slow cooker.

3. Stir in the vegetable stock, onions, potatoes, carrots, celery, mushrooms, basil, thyme, and bay leaves.

4. Cover and cook on low for 6 to 7 hours or on high for 4 hours.

5. Remove the bay leaves.

6. Ladle the stew into bowls and serve hot with the pineapple on the side, if desired.

Sweet and Spicy Chickpea Stew

MAKES 4 SERVINGS

*Sweet and Spicy Chickpea Stew and Slow-Cooked Brown Basmati Rice (page 22)
are a food match made in heaven. Starchy and bold, the chickpeas and the rice
compete for center stage in this healthful, hearty meal, but the combination of
flavors is complementary.*

2 (15-OUNCE) CANS CHICKPEAS, RINSED AND DRAINED

3½ CUPS WATER

1 CUP CHOPPED BROCCOLI FLORETS

1 MEDIUM YELLOW ONION, COARSELY CHOPPED

1 SWEET POTATO, PEELED AND CUT INTO BITE-SIZE PIECES

1 SMALL CARROT, SLICED

1 CELERY STALK, SLICED

1 SMALL LEEK, SLICED

1½ TEASPOONS FRESH LEMON JUICE

1½ TEASPOONS SOY SAUCE

1 TEASPOON PREPARED HORSERADISH

½ TEASPOON GROUND CORIANDER

¼ TEASPOON GROUND CUMIN

1 DASH HOT SAUCE

PINCH OF CAYENNE PEPPER

1. Combine the chickpeas, water, broccoli, onion, sweet potato, carrot, celery,
leek, lemon juice, and soy sauce in the slow cooker.

2. Stir in the horseradish, coriander, cumin, hot sauce, and cayenne pepper.

3. Cover and cook on low for 6 to 8 hours, or until vegetables are tender.

4. Ladle the stew into bowls and serve hot.

Creamy Curry Stew

MAKES 6 TO 8 SERVINGS

Coconut milk and a little puréeing are what make this curry stew seem almost milky. Coconut milk provides a creamy consistency unparalleled by cow's milk and certainly without all the complications. This milk provides a portion of your recommended daily intake for calcium, along with vitamins B, C, and E, and phosphorus, iron, selenium, and magnesium. Magnesium calms the nerves and can lead to lower blood pressure. Serve with Slow-Cooked Brown Basmati Rice (page 22).

1 (15-OUNCE) CAN CHICKPEAS, RINSED AND DRAINED

3 CUPS CHOPPED CAULIFLOWER FLORETS

1 POUND WHITE POTATOES, PEELED AND CUT INTO 1-INCH PIECES

1½ CUPS SLICED CARROTS

¾ CUP COARSELY CHOPPED RED BELL PEPPER

½ CUP CHOPPED YELLOW ONION

2 TEASPOONS GRATED FRESH GINGER

2 TO 3 TEASPOONS CURRY POWDER

½ TEASPOON SEA SALT

⅛ TEASPOON RED PEPPER FLAKES

3½ CUPS VEGETABLE STOCK (PAGE 20)

1 (14-OUNCE) CAN UNSWEETENED COCONUT MILK

CHOPPED FRESH CILANTRO, FOR GARNISH

1. Combine the chickpeas, cauliflower, potatoes, carrots, red bell pepper, and onion in the slow cooker.

2. Sprinkle the vegetables with the ginger, curry powder, sea salt, and red pepper flakes.

3. Pour the vegetable stock over the vegetables and spices.

4. Cover and cook on low for 8 to 10 hours or on high for 4 to 5 hours.

5. Remove 1 cup of vegetables from the slow cooker.

continued ▶

6. Purée the vegetables in a blender or food processor.

7. Add the puréed vegetables back to the slow cooker.

8. Stir in the coconut milk just before serving.

9. Ladle the stew into bowls, garnish with the fresh cilantro, and serve hot.

Creamy Pumpkin Stew

MAKES 4 SERVINGS

Pumpkin is often overlooked in everyday cooking due to the popularity of its better-known cousins, butternut squash and acorn squash. Pumpkins come in a variety of shapes, sizes, and types. Many types of pumpkins are ideal for cooking and baking. Japanese, Queensland blue, and golden nugget are just a few of the varieties available in the marketplace. This stew really hits the spot when served with a green salad and warm bread.

4 CUPS VEGETABLE STOCK (PAGE 20)
1 CUP FROZEN CORN
1 CUP UNSWEETENED COCONUT MILK
½ CUP CANNED PUMPKIN PURÉE
1 MEDIUM WHITE POTATO, PEELED AND DICED
2 GARLIC CLOVES, MINCED
1 TEASPOON DRIED THYME
1 BAY LEAF
CAYENNE PEPPER, TO TASTE
SEA SALT AND CRACKED BLACK PEPPER, TO TASTE

1. Pour the vegetable stock into the slow cooker.

2. Stir in the corn, coconut milk, pumpkin purée, potato, garlic, thyme, bay leaf, and cayenne pepper.

3. Cover and cook on low for 6 to 8 hours or on high for 3 to 4 hours.

4. Remove the bay leaf.

5. Purée the stew using a handheld immersion blender. Keep the blender's head below the soup's surface and purée as little or as much as desired.

6. Season with the sea salt and black pepper.

7. Ladle the stew into bowls and serve hot.

Veggie and Squash Stew

MAKES 4 TO 6 SERVINGS

A good stew can be a hearty meal, and this stew certainly fits the bill. Thicker than soup, this nutrient-dense stew also provides greater satiety. The root vegetables supply an abundance of vitamins and minerals, the chickpeas supply the protein, and the whole grain supplies the dietary fiber.

1 (14½-OUNCE) CAN DICED TOMATOES, UNDRAINED
1 CUP VEGETABLE STOCK (PAGE 20)
1 CUP CUBED BUTTERNUT SQUASH
1 CUP COOKED OR CANNED CHICKPEAS, RINSED AND DRAINED
½ CUP CHOPPED ZUCCHINI
2 MEDIUM CARROTS, CHOPPED
1 SMALL YELLOW ONION, CHOPPED
1 GARLIC CLOVE, MINCED
½ TEASPOON GROUND CUMIN
¼ TEASPOON GROUND ALLSPICE
⅛ TEASPOON CRACKED BLACK PEPPER
2 CUPS HOT COOKED COUSCOUS
CRUMBLED VEGAN FETA CHEESE

1. Combine the tomatoes with their juices, vegetable stock, butternut squash, chickpeas, zucchini, carrots, onion, and garlic in the slow cooker.

2. Stir in the cumin, allspice, and black pepper.

3. Cover and cook on low for 7 to 9 hours, or until the vegetables are tender.

4. Ladle the stew into bowls over the couscous, top with the vegan feta cheese, and serve hot.

Black Bean and Chipotle Pepper Stew

MAKES 6 TO 8 SERVINGS

Chipotle peppers are ripe red jalapeño peppers that have been smoked and dried. Chipotle literally means "smoked chili." The vast majority of these peppers come from Chihuahua, a state in northern Mexico.

4 (15-OUNCE) CANS BLACK BEANS, RINSED AND DRAINED

1 (28-OUNCE) CAN DICED TOMATOES, UNDRAINED

3 CUPS VEGETABLE STOCK (PAGE 20)

¾ CUP UNCOOKED QUINOA, RINSED

1 LARGE RED ONION, DICED

1 LARGE GREEN BELL PEPPER, SEEDED AND CHOPPED

1 LARGE RED BELL PEPPER, SEEDED AND CHOPPED

3 GARLIC CLOVES, MINCED

1 OR 2 CHIPOTLE PEPPERS

2 TEASPOONS CHILI POWDER

1 TEASPOON GROUND CORIANDER

½ TEASPOON GROUND CINNAMON

SEA SALT AND CRACKED BLACK PEPPER, TO TASTE

CHOPPED FRESH CILANTRO, FOR GARNISH

DICED AVOCADO (OPTIONAL)

1. Combine the beans, tomatoes with their juices, vegetable stock, quinoa, onion, green and red bell peppers, garlic, and chipotle peppers in the slow cooker.

2. Stir in the chili powder, coriander, cinnamon, sea salt, and black pepper.

3. Cover and cook on low for 6 to 8 hours or on high for 4 hours.

4. Remove the chipotle peppers.

5. Ladle the stew into bowls, garnish with the fresh cilantro, and serve hot with diced avocado, if desired.

Lentil and Bean Stew

MAKES 4 TO 5 SERVINGS

If you're looking for a really high-protein stew, you've come to the right place. This stew is made from two types of chickpeas, red lentils, and quinoa (which is a complete protein), not to mention all the veggies and mushrooms. Looking for even more? Add some walnuts and crumbled vegan beef to the mix.

5 CUPS VEGETABLE STOCK (PAGE 20)

1 (28-OUNCE) CAN DICED TOMATOES WITH BASIL AND
    GARLIC, UNDRAINED

1 (8-OUNCE) CAN TOMATO SAUCE

1 CUP COOKED OR CANNED WHITE CHICKPEAS, RINSED AND DRAINED

1 CUP COOKED OR CANNED GREEN CHICKPEAS, RINSED AND DRAINED

¾ CUP DRIED RED LENTILS, RINSED

½ CUP UNCOOKED QUINOA, RINSED

4 LARGE CARROTS, PEELED AND CHOPPED

2 TO 3 MEDIUM ZUCCHINI, SLICED

1 SMALL SWEET POTATO, PEELED AND CHOPPED

1½ CUPS WHITE ONION, CHOPPED

¾ CUP FROZEN CORN

¾ CUP FROZEN PEAS

½ CUP DICED WHITE MUSHROOMS

3 GARLIC CLOVES, MINCED

5 TABLESPOONS VEGAN WORCESTERSHIRE SAUCE

3 TABLESPOONS SOY SAUCE

1 TEASPOON DRIED ITALIAN SEASONING

SEA SALT AND CRACKED BLACK PEPPER, TO TASTE

3 HEAPING TABLESPOONS CORNSTARCH DISSOLVED IN
    ¼ CUP COLD WATER

1. Pour the vegetable stock into the slow cooker.

2. Stir in the tomatoes with their juices, tomato sauce, white and green chickpeas, red lentils, quinoa, carrots, zucchini, sweet potato, onion, corn,

peas, white mushrooms, garlic, vegan Worcestershire sauce, soy sauce, Italian seasoning, sea salt, and black pepper.

3. Stir the cornstarch mixture into the ingredients in the slow cooker.

4. Cover and cook on low for 6 to 8 hours or on high for 4 hours.

5. Ladle the stew into bowls and serve hot.

Mexican-Style Dumpling Stew

MAKES 4 TO 6 SERVINGS

Dumplings bring this Mexican-style stew to an entirely different level. The foundation of a good dumpling is flour, potatoes, or bread. (Animal products are sometimes included, too, but these dumplings are animal-friendly.) Dumplings are traditionally cooked by frying or baking, and now slow-cooking can be added to the list. Serve with a side of lightly steamed collard greens for added flavor and nutrients.

FOR THE SOUP:

3 CUPS VEGETABLE STOCK (PAGE 20)

2 (10-OUNCE) CANS MEXICAN-STYLE CHOPPED TOMATOES, UNDRAINED

1 (15-OUNCE) CAN KIDNEY BEANS, RINSED AND DRAINED

1 (15-OUNCE) CAN BLACK BEANS, RINSED AND DRAINED

1¼ CUPS FROZEN CORN

1 CUP CHOPPED YELLOW ONION

1 (4-OUNCE) CAN CHOPPED GREEN CHILES, DRAINED

2 LARGE CARROTS, SLICED

3 GARLIC CLOVES, MINCED

1½ TEASPOONS CHILI POWDER

HOT SAUCE, TO TASTE

FOR THE DUMPLINGS:

⅓ CUP ALL-PURPOSE FLOUR

¼ CUP CORNMEAL

1 TEASPOON BAKING POWDER

PINCH OF SEA SALT

PINCH OF CRACKED BLACK PEPPER

2½ TABLESPOONS SOY MILK

1 TABLESPOON VEGETABLE OIL

Make the soup:

1. Pour the vegetable stock into the slow cooker.

2. Stir in the tomatoes with their juices, kidney beans, black beans, corn, onion, chiles, carrots, garlic, chili powder, and hot sauce.

3. Cover and cook on low for 8 to 10 hours.

Make the dumplings:

1. In a large bowl, combine the flour, cornmeal, baking powder, salt, and black pepper.

2. In a small bowl, combine the soy milk and the vegetable oil.

3. Add the soy milk and vegetable oil to the flour mixture and stir until just moistened.

4. Turn the slow cooker to high and drop the dumpling batter by the teaspoonful on top of the stew.

5. Cover and cook for 30 to 40 minutes, or until the dumplings are cooked.

6. Ladle the stew into bowls and serve hot.

"Meaty" Shiitake Stew

MAKES 4 TO 6 SERVINGS

Shiitake mushrooms are often thought of as the meat of the vegan diet. They originated from East Asia and are used in many forms of traditional medicine. They are credited with enhancing the immune system, decreasing the risk of blood clots, and possessing antibacterial and antiviral properties. This stew goes nicely with a side of lightly steamed kale.

1 (14½-OUNCE) CAN DICED TOMATOES, UNDRAINED
1¼ CUPS VEGETABLE STOCK (PAGE 20)
1 POUND VEGAN BEEF, CHOPPED OR CRUMBLED
8 OUNCES FRESH SHIITAKE MUSHROOMS, STEMS REMOVED
    AND CAPS SLICED
½ CUP CHOPPED WHITE ONION
10 SMALL NEW POTATOES, QUARTERED
3 LARGE CARROTS, CHOPPED
1 TABLESPOON SOY SAUCE
1 TEASPOON SUGAR
1 TEASPOON DRIED MARJORAM
SEA SALT AND CRACKED BLACK PEPPER, TO TASTE

1. Combine the tomatoes with their juices, vegetable stock, vegan beef, shiitake mushrooms, onion, potatoes, carrots, soy sauce, sugar, and marjoram in the slow cooker.

2. Season with the sea salt and black pepper and stir.

3. Cover and cook on low for 6 to 8 hours, or until the potatoes are tender.

4. Ladle the stew into bowls and serve hot.

Two-Bean Chili

MAKES 6 SERVINGS

While pinto beans and kidney beans differ in shape and size, they have more things in common than they have differences. Both types of beans are excellent sources of fiber and iron, with kidney beans supplying a little bit more of each. Even so, pinto beans are credited with being the most consumed bean in the United States. If you prefer pinto beans to kidney beans, just replace the kidney beans in this chili with more pintos and enjoy.

1 (15-OUNCE) CAN KIDNEY BEANS, RINSED AND DRAINED

1 (15-OUNCE) CAN PINTO BEANS, RINSED AND DRAINED

1 (14½-OUNCE) CAN DICED TOMATOES, UNDRAINED

1 (4-OUNCE) CAN CHOPPED GREEN CHILES, DRAINED

1 CUP FINELY CHOPPED YELLOW ONIONS

1 CUP FINELY CHOPPED CARROTS

½ CUP FINELY CHOPPED RED BELL PEPPER

½ CUP FINELY CHOPPED GREEN BELL PEPPER

1 GARLIC CLOVE, MINCED

¾ CUP FRESH ORANGE JUICE

¾ CUP WATER

4 TEASPOONS CHILI POWDER

1 TEASPOON GROUND CUMIN

1 TABLESPOON CORNSTARCH DISSOLVED IN 2 TABLESPOONS COLD WATER

CHOPPED FRESH CILANTRO, FOR GARNISH

1. Combine the kidney beans, pinto beans, tomatoes with their juices, green chiles, onions, carrots, red and green bell peppers, garlic, orange juice, and ¾ cup of the water in the slow cooker.

2. Stir in the chili powder and cumin.

3. Cover and cook on low for 6 to 8 hours or on high for 4 hours.

4. Stir the cornstarch mixture into the slow cooker 30 minutes before serving.

5. Ladle the chili into bowls and garnish with the fresh cilantro.

Black Bean and Tomato Chili

MAKES 4 SERVINGS

This black bean chili has few ingredients but plenty of flavor. Black beans and tomatoes are a highly agreeable combination; when joined by cocoa powder, they become irresistible. The cocoa powder builds on the antioxidant properties of the black beans and tomatoes and adds a smooth roasted flavor.

2 (15-OUNCE) CANS BLACK BEANS, RINSED AND DRAINED

2 (14½-OUNCE) CANS DICED TOMATOES, UNDRAINED

¼ CUP WATER

1 MEDIUM RED ONION, DICED

1 TABLESPOON UNSWEETENED COCOA POWDER

¼ TEASPOON SEA SALT

¼ TEASPOON CHILI POWDER

VEGAN SOUR CREAM (OPTIONAL)

SHREDDED VEGAN CHEDDAR CHEESE (OPTIONAL)

CHOPPED FRESH CILANTRO, FOR GARNISH

1. Combine the beans, tomatoes with their juices, water, onion, and cocoa powder in the slow cooker.

2. Stir in the sea salt and chili powder.

3. Cover and cook on low for 4 to 5 hours or on high for 2 to 3 hours.

4. Ladle the chili into bowls, top with the vegan sour cream and shredded vegan cheddar cheese (if desired), garnish with the fresh cilantro, and serve hot.

Black-Eyed Pea Chili

Whether you call them black-eyed beans, field peas, or cow fodder, black-eyed peas are considered a symbol of prosperity in the South and are served to celebrate the New Year. Black-eyed peas provide potassium, iron, folate, fiber, and protein to your diet and are virtually fat-free. Black-eyed peas go great with freshly baked cornbread, and so does this chili.

1 (15-OUNCE) CAN BLACK-EYED PEAS, RINSED AND DRAINED

1 (15-OUNCE) CAN NAVY BEANS, RINSED AND DRAINED

1 CUP VEGETABLE STOCK (PAGE 20)

1 LARGE YELLOW ONION, CHOPPED

1 CUP FROZEN CORN

1 CUP DICED TOMATOES

½ CUP CHOPPED SCALLIONS

½ CUP TOMATO PASTE

¼ CUP DICED CANNED JALAPEÑO PEPPERS

1 TEASPOON PREPARED MUSTARD

2 TEASPOONS CHILI POWDER

½ TEASPOON GROUND CUMIN

¼ TEASPOON DRIED OREGANO

1. Combine the black-eyed peas, beans, vegetable stock, yellow onion, corn, tomatoes, scallions, tomato paste, and jalapeño peppers in the slow cooker.

2. Stir in the mustard, chili powder, cumin, and oregano.

3. Cover and cook on low for 8 to 10 hours or on high for 4 to 5 hours.

4. Ladle the chili into bowls and serve hot.

Baked Bean Chili

MAKES 8 SERVINGS

Baked beans are reminiscent of backyard barbecues and picnics. This chili inspires the same feelings of fun with family and friends. Throw an outdoor party, dish up some Baked Bean Chili, and serve with veggie dogs and all the fixings to build a whole new set of memories.

1 CAN VEGETARIAN BAKED BEANS, UNDRAINED

1 (15-OUNCE) CAN BLACK BEANS, RINSED AND DRAINED

1 (15-OUNCE) CAN KIDNEY BEANS, RINSED AND DRAINED

1 (15-OUNCE) CAN CHICKPEAS, RINSED AND DRAINED

2 (14½-OUNCE) CANS STEWED TOMATOES

2 CELERY STALKS, CHOPPED

1 LARGE GREEN BELL PEPPER, SEEDED AND CHOPPED

1 LARGE YELLOW ONION, CHOPPED

1 TABLESPOON CHILI POWDER

1 TABLESPOON DRIED BASIL

1 TABLESPOON DRIED OREGANO

1 TABLESPOON DRIED PARSLEY

1. Combine the baked beans with their juices, black beans, kidney beans, chickpeas, stewed tomatoes, celery, bell pepper, and onion in the slow cooker.

2. Stir in the chili powder, basil, oregano and parsley.

3. Cover and cook on high for 3 hours.

4. Ladle the chili into bowls and serve hot.

Lima Bean Chili

MAKES 4 TO 6 SERVINGS

Beans are the foundation of a good chili, and these can even include lima beans. Just as beneficial to your health as other beans, lima beans also contain the trace mineral molybdenum in high enough amounts to help the body break down sulfites. Sulfites are a commonly used food preservative and can be found in wine, salad bars, and myriad other places in the food system. Many people suffer from sulfite side effects and could greatly benefit from more lima beans in their diet.

4 CUPS VEGETABLE STOCK (PAGE 20)

1 (28-OUNCE) CAN DICED TOMATOES, UNDRAINED

1 (15-OUNCE) CAN BLACK BEANS, RINSED AND DRAINED

1 (15-OUNCE) CAN WHITE BEANS, RINSED AND DRAINED

1 (15-OUNCE) CAN RED KIDNEY BEANS, RINSED AND DRAINED

1 CUP FROZEN BABY LIMA BEANS

1 CUP CHOPPED YELLOW ONION

1 LARGE GREEN BELL PEPPER, SEEDED AND CHOPPED

2 GARLIC CLOVES, MINCED

1 TABLESPOON MINCED PICKLED JALAPEÑO

1 TO 2 TEASPOONS HOT SAUCE

2 TABLESPOONS CHILI POWDER

2 TABLESPOONS DRIED OREGANO

2 TEASPOONS GROUND CUMIN

1 TEASPOON GROUND CORIANDER

⅓ CUP UNCOOKED COUSCOUS

SEA SALT AND CRACKED BLACK PEPPER, TO TASTE

CHOPPED FRESH CILANTRO, FOR GARNISH

1. Pour the vegetable stock into the slow cooker.

2. Stir in the tomatoes with their juices, black beans, white beans, kidney beans, lima beans, onion, bell pepper, garlic, jalapeño, hot sauce, chili powder, oregano, cumin, and coriander.

continued ▶

3. Cover and cook on low for 6 to 8 hours or on high for 3 to 4 hours.

4. Add the couscous, sea salt, and black pepper at the end of the cooking process and continue cooking for 15 minutes, or until the couscous is tender.

5. Ladle the chili into soup bowls, garnish with the fresh cilantro, and serve hot.

Spicy Vegan Chili

Meatless chili contains plenty of protein and nutrients, but without all the cholesterol, saturated fat, and calories of meat. Using dried beans is always an option; however, this meatless version contains so many beans that using canned beans makes it a lot easier. Either way, your chili will be a hit.

2 (15-OUNCE) CANS BLACK BEANS, RINSED AND DRAINED

1 (15-OUNCE) CAN PINTO BEANS, RINSED AND DRAINED

1 (15-OUNCE) CAN KIDNEY BEANS, RINSED AND DRAINED

2 (14½-OUNCE) CANS DICED TOMATOES, UNDRAINED

1¾ CUPS VEGETABLE STOCK (PAGE 20)

1 CUP CHOPPED YELLOW ONION

¼ CUP SEEDED AND CHOPPED JALAPEÑO PEPPER

2 GARLIC CLOVES, MINCED

2 TEASPOONS VEGAN WORCESTERSHIRE SAUCE

2 TEASPOONS CHILI POWDER

2 TEASPOONS GROUND CUMIN

½ TEASPOON SEA SALT

VEGAN SOUR CREAM (OPTIONAL)

SHREDDED VEGAN MONTEREY JACK CHEESE (OPTIONAL)

CHOPPED FRESH CILANTRO, FOR GARNISH

1. Combine the black beans, pinto beans, kidney beans, tomatoes with their juices, vegetable stock, onion, jalapeño pepper, garlic, and vegan Worcestershire sauce in the slow cooker.

2. Stir in the chili powder, cumin, and salt.

3. Cover and cook on low for 8 hours.

4. Ladle the chili into bowls, top with the vegan sour cream and vegan Monterey Jack cheese (if desired), garnish with the fresh cilantro, and serve hot.

Sweet Potato Chili

MAKES 4 TO 6 SERVINGS

Starchy and sweet, this deep orange potato is a refreshing change from the white potatoes often found in chili. In addition to the manganese, vitamins C and E, and beta carotene in sweet potatoes, vitamin B6 is the sweet potato's claim to fame. Vitamin B6 is necessary for decreasing the body's homocysteine, a non-protein amino acid that is responsible for hardening of the arteries and is a valuable marker for cardiovascular disease.

1 (28-OUNCE) CAN DICED FIRE-ROASTED TOMATOES, UNDRAINED

1 (15-OUNCE) CAN BLACK BEANS, RINSED AND DRAINED

1 (15-OUNCE) CAN KIDNEY BEANS, RINSED AND DRAINED

1 CUP WATER

1 MEDIUM SWEET POTATO, PEELED AND CUT INTO ½-INCH PIECES

1 MEDIUM RED ONION, CHOPPED

1 LARGE GREEN BELL PEPPER, SEEDED AND CHOPPED

4 GARLIC CLOVES, CHOPPED

1 TABLESPOON CHILI POWDER

1 TABLESPOON GROUND CUMIN

2 TEASPOONS UNSWEETENED COCOA POWDER

¼ TEASPOON GROUND CINNAMON

SEA SALT AND CRACKED BLACK PEPPER, TO TASTE

VEGAN SOUR CREAM (OPTIONAL)

BAKED CORN CHIPS (OPTIONAL)

1. Combine the tomatoes with their juices, black beans, kidney beans, water, sweet potato, red onion, green bell pepper, and garlic in the slow cooker.

2. Stir in the chili powder, cumin, cocoa, cinnamon, sea salt, and black pepper.

3. Cover and cook on low for 7 to 8 hours or on high for 4 to 5 hours, or until the sweet potatoes are tender and the chili has thickened.

4. Ladle the chili into bowls, top with the vegan sour cream (if using), and serve hot with baked corn chips, if desired.

Quinoa Chili

Quinoa (KEEN-wa) might be difficult to spell, but it's certainly easy to eat. Called the "mother grain" by the Incas, this ancient grain is actually a seed and is referred to as an alternative grain in the gluten-free community. In addition to being gluten-free, quinoa is a complete high-quality protein and is also easy to digest.

3 CUPS VEGETABLE STOCK (PAGE 20)

1 (15-OUNCE) CAN KIDNEY BEANS, RINSED AND DRAINED

1 (15-OUNCE) CAN BLACK BEANS, RINSED AND DRAINED

1½ CUPS UNCOOKED QUINOA, RINSED

1 (8-OUNCE) CAN TOMATO SAUCE

¼ CUP CHOPPED YELLOW ONION

1 CELERY STALK, DICED

½ LARGE GREEN BELL PEPPER, SEEDED AND DICED

½ LARGE RED BELL PEPPER, SEEDED AND DICED

2 TABLESPOONS MINCED JALAPEÑO PEPPER

1 TABLESPOON MINCED GARLIC

1 TABLESPOON OLIVE OIL

2 TEASPOONS GROUND CORIANDER

1 TEASPOON GROUND CUMIN

1 TEASPOON PAPRIKA

1 TEASPOON DRIED BASIL

½ TEASPOON DRIED THYME

½ TEASPOON DRIED MARJORAM

⅛ TEASPOON CHIPOTLE PEPPER POWDER

1 BAY LEAF

1 TABLESPOON LIGHT MOLASSES

1 TABLESPOON SOY SAUCE

CRACKED BLACK PEPPER, TO TASTE

VEGAN SOUR CREAM (OPTIONAL)

CHOPPED FRESH CILANTRO, FOR GARNISH

continued ▶

Quinoa Chili *continued* ▶

1. Combine the vegetable stock, kidney beans, black beans, quinoa, tomato sauce, onion, celery, green and red bell peppers, jalapeño pepper, garlic, and olive oil in the slow cooker.

2. Stir in the coriander, cumin, paprika, basil, thyme, marjoram, chipotle pepper powder, and bay leaf.

3. Cover and cook on low for 5 to 6 hours.

4. Remove the bay leaf.

5. Stir in the molasses, soy sauce, and black pepper.

6. Ladle the chili into bowls, top with the vegan sour cream (if using), garnish with the fresh cilantro, and serve hot.

Spicy Pumpkin Chili

MAKES 4 TO 6 SERVINGS

The chili sauce and chili powder make it spicy enough for the average chili eater. If you're above average, just keep adding the heat until you're satisfied. The pumpkin purée and pumpkin pie spice contribute a mildly sweet and smooth flavor.

1 (28-OUNCE) CAN DICED STEWED TOMATOES

1 (15-OUNCE) CAN KIDNEY BEANS, RINSED AND DRAINED

1 CUP CANNED PUMPKIN PURÉE

1 (12-OUNCE) BAG FROZEN VEGAN CRUMBLES

1 MEDIUM YELLOW ONION, CHOPPED

1 (12-OUNCE) BOTTLE CHILI SAUCE

1 TO 2 TABLESPOONS CHILI POWDER

2 TEASPOONS PUMPKIN PIE SPICE

1½ TEASPOONS SEA SALT

1 TEASPOON CRACKED BLACK PEPPER

1. Combine the tomatoes, beans, pumpkin purée, vegan crumbles, onion, and chili sauce in the slow cooker.

2. Stir in the chili powder, pumpkin pie spice, sea salt, and black pepper.

3. Cover and cook on low for 3 to 4 hours.

4. Ladle the chili into soup bowls and serve hot.

Great Northern Bean "Chicken" Chili

MAKES 6 TO 8 SERVINGS

There is some debate within the vegan community about whether eating faux meat is a desirable activity. For those who miss meat, vegan chicken strips add a real boost to this white bean soup. For those who don't care for faux meats, this soup may just change their mind. Serve lightly steamed greens alongside for a complete meal.

6 CUPS VEGETABLE STOCK (PAGE 20)

1 (15-OUNCE) CAN GREAT NORTHERN BEANS, RINSED AND DRAINED

2 (4-OUNCE) CANS CHOPPED MILD GREEN CHILES, DRAINED

1 LARGE YELLOW ONION, CHOPPED

3 GARLIC CLOVES, MINCED

1 TABLESPOON NUTRITIONAL YEAST

2 TEASPOONS GROUND CUMIN

1½ TEASPOONS DRIED OREGANO

1 TEASPOON SEA SALT

½ TEASPOON CAYENNE PEPPER

¼ TEASPOON GROUND CLOVES

CRACKED BLACK PEPPER, TO TASTE

1 (10-OUNCE) PACKAGE VEGAN CHICKEN STRIPS, COOKED
    AND FINELY DICED

1. Pour the vegetable stock into the slow cooker.

2. Stir in the beans, green chiles, onion, garlic, nutritional yeast, cumin, oregano, sea salt, cayenne pepper, cloves, and black pepper.

3. Cover and cook on low for 6 to 8 hours or on high for 4 to 6 hours.

4. Stir the vegan chicken strips into the chili 1 hour before serving.

5. Ladle the chili into bowls and serve hot.

CHAPTER SEVEN

Beans and Grains

FARRO AND SPLIT PEA SOUP

MANDARIN ORANGE
   VEGETABLES AND RICE

SPINACH AND YELLOW RICE

SPANISH RICE AND BLACK BEANS

MEXICAN BEANS AND RICE

CAJUN-STYLE KIDNEY BEANS
   AND RICE

CHICKPEA COUSCOUS

BARLEY AND BEANS

BEANS AND MOLASSES

GRAINS WITH SESAME SEEDS

MEXICAN BLACK-EYED PEAS

BEAN SMORGASBORD

SPICY LENTILS

SLOW-COOKED STUFFING

LENTIL PASTA SAUCE

MAC AND CHEESE

MACARONI CASSEROLE
   FLORENTINE

VEGAN RISOTTO

SPAGHETTI AND HOT DOGS

SOUTHERN-STYLE CASSEROLE

LIMA BEAN GUMBO

Beans and Grains

Farro and Split Pea Soup

Most of the farro sold in this country is whole-grain emmer wheat imported from Italy. Emmer retains much of its original fiber and nutrients, including B vitamins, manganese, and zinc. Slightly chewy and a little nutty, farro is a welcome addition to any pantry and any meal.

4 CUPS WATER

4 CUPS VEGETABLE STOCK (PAGE 20)

2 CUPS CHOPPED TURNIPS

1½ CUPS UNCOOKED FARRO

1 CUP DRIED SPLIT PEAS

2 TEASPOONS GARAM MASALA

2 TEASPOONS SMOKED PAPRIKA

1 TEASPOON GROUND TURMERIC

3 BAY LEAVES

SEA SALT AND CRACKED BLACK PEPPER, TO TASTE

TOASTED WHOLE-GRAIN BREAD (OPTIONAL)

1. Pour the water and vegetable stock into the slow cooker.

2. Stir in the turnips, farro, split peas, garam masala, paprika, turmeric, and bay leaves.

3. Cover and cook on low for 8 to 10 hours or on high for 3 to 4 hours.

4. Season with the sea salt and black pepper.

5. Ladle the soup into bowls and serve hot with the toasted whole-grain bread, if desired.

Mandarin Orange Vegetables and Rice

MAKES 4 TO 6 SERVINGS

Mandarin oranges are special members of the orange family for several reasons. They are easy to peel, and one mandarin orange can supply as much as 80 percent of your recommended daily intake of vitamin C. They are also a good source of vitamin A, dietary fiber, calcium, magnesium, and potassium.

2 CUPS CHOPPED BROCCOLI FLORETS

1½ CUPS THINLY SLICED YELLOW SQUASH

1½ CUPS THINLY SLICED ZUCCHINI

1 CUP HALVED BABY CARROTS

1 (8-OUNCE) CAN MANDARIN ORANGES, UNDRAINED

3 TABLESPOONS MINCED FRESH GINGER

2 GARLIC CLOVES, MINCED

SLOW-COOKED BROWN BASMATI RICE (PAGE 22)

1. Combine the broccoli, squash, zucchini, carrots, mandarin oranges with their juices, ginger, and garlic in the slow cooker and stir well.

2. Cover and cook on low for 8 to 10 hours.

3. Serve hot with the rice.

Spinach and Yellow Rice

MAKES 6 TO 8 SERVINGS

Saffron, a spice that was originally grown in ancient Egypt, is now produced in several countries, but most of it comes from Spain. Saffron gives white rice a yellow hue from the herb's crocin content (a carotenoid dye). It also imparts a hint of sweetness to food. Serve this dish with lightly steamed kale or collard greens.

4 CUPS VEGETABLE STOCK (PAGE 20)

2 CUPS UNCOOKED CONVERTED WHITE RICE

1 (10-OUNCE) PACKAGE FROZEN CHOPPED SPINACH, THAWED, UNDRAINED

1 LARGE YELLOW ONION, CHOPPED

1 LARGE GREEN BELL PEPPER, SEEDED AND CHOPPED

2 GARLIC CLOVES, MINCED

¾ CUP CHOPPED ROASTED RED PEPPER

½ TEASPOON SAFFRON THREADS

½ TEASPOON GROUND CUMIN

½ TEASPOON SEA SALT

¼ TEASPOON CRACKED BLACK PEPPER

⅛ TEASPOON CAYENNE PEPPER

1 (16-OUNCE) BAG FROZEN MIXED VEGETABLES, THAWED

1 (6-OUNCE) CAN ARTICHOKE HEARTS, RINSED, DRAINED,
    AND QUARTERED

1. Pour the vegetable stock into the slow cooker.

2. Stir in the white rice, spinach, onion, bell pepper, garlic, roasted red pepper, saffron, cumin, sea salt, black pepper, and cayenne pepper.

3. Cover and cook on low for 4 hours, or until the rice is just tender but the grains are still separate and not mushy.

4. Stir in the mixed vegetables and artichokes.

5. Leave uncovered and cook on high for an additional 10 minutes.

6. Serve immediately.

Spanish Rice and Black Beans

Spanish rice is made from white rice, tomatoes, garlic, and onions. This recipe fills the bill but kicks it up a notch by using brown basmati rice. Brown rice is a whole grain, high in fiber, and when consumed on a regular basis, helps lower the risk of many types of chronic disease. The black beans magnify the health benefits of the brown rice and complement the flavors of this dish perfectly.

1 (15-OUNCE) CAN TOMATO SAUCE

1½ CUPS WATER

¾ CUP UNCOOKED LONG-GRAIN BROWN BASMATI RICE

1 MEDIUM YELLOW ONION, DICED

1 MEDIUM GREEN BELL PEPPER, SEEDED AND FINELY CHOPPED

2 TOMATOES, PEELED AND QUARTERED

2 TABLESPOONS SALSA

2 TEASPOONS VEGAN WORCESTERSHIRE SAUCE

2 TEASPOONS CHILI POWDER

½ TEASPOONS GARLIC POWDER

SLOW-COOKED BLACK BEANS (PAGE 26) OR 2 TO 3 (15-OUNCE) CANS
    BLACK BEANS, RINSED AND DRAINED, HEATED

1. Combine the tomato sauce, water, brown rice, onion, bell pepper, tomatoes, salsa, vegan Worcestershire sauce, chili powder, and garlic powder in the slow cooker and stir well.

2. Cover and cook on low for 7 to 8 hours.

3. Serve hot with the black beans.

Mexican Beans and Rice

MAKES 6 SERVINGS

Beans and rice have been a long-time staple of vegan diets. Together they supply protein and carbohydrates, as well as great taste and satiety factor. Why not try beans and rice Mexican style? Serve with toasted tortillas and you have dinner.

1 (15-OUNCE) CAN KIDNEY BEANS, RINSED AND DRAINED

1 (10-OUNCE) CAN MEXICAN-STYLE DICED TOMATOES, UNDRAINED

1 (8-OUNCE) CAN TOMATO SAUCE

1 CUP WATER MIXED WITH 1 TABLESPOON TOMATO PASTE

½ CUP UNCOOKED LONG-GRAIN BROWN BASMATI RICE

½ CUP CHOPPED YELLOW ONION

1 TABLESPOON MINCED GARLIC

1 TABLESPOON MAPLE SYRUP

1 CANNED CHIPOTLE PEPPER IN ADOBO SAUCE, CHOPPED

2 TEASPOONS DRIED OREGANO

½ TEASPOON SMOKED PAPRIKA

PINCH OF CINNAMON

1 BAY LEAF

1. Combine the kidney beans, tomatoes with their juices, tomato sauce, water mixed with tomato paste, brown rice, onion, garlic, and maple syrup in the slow cooker and stir well.

2. Stir in the chipotle, oregano, paprika, cinnamon, and bay leaf.

3. Cover and cook on low for 6 hours, or until the rice is cooked.

4. Remove the bay leaf.

5. Serve hot.

Cajun-Style Kidney Beans and Rice

MAKES 4 TO 6 SERVINGS

Many Cajun meals include three different components: beans, rice, and a vegetable. Adding a side of lightly steamed collard greens to the beans and rice in this recipe rounds out the meal nicely.

4 (15-OUNCE) CANS KIDNEY BEANS, RINSED AND DRAINED

1 CUP WATER

4 GARLIC CLOVES, MINCED

2 TEASPOONS SALT-FREE CAJUN SEASONING

A FEW DROPS LIQUID SMOKE

4 BAY LEAVES

SEA SALT AND CRACKED BLACK PEPPER, TO TASTE

SLOW-COOKED BROWN BASMATI RICE (PAGE 22)

HOT SAUCE (OPTIONAL)

1. Combine the beans and the water in the slow cooker.

2. Stir in the garlic, Cajun seasoning, liquid smoke, bay leaves, sea salt, and black pepper.

3. Cover and cook on low for 6 to 8 hours.

4. Serve hot over the rice with a dash of hot sauce, if desired.

Chickpea Couscous

MAKES 8 SERVINGS

A durum wheat product made from semolina, couscous is a familiar food throughout North Africa and western Sicily. Chickpeas are commonly served with couscous to add even more protein and substance.

1 (15-OUNCE) CAN CHICKPEAS, RINSED AND DRAINED

1 (14½-OUNCE) CAN DICED TOMATOES, UNDRAINED

1 CUP VEGETABLE STOCK (PAGE 20)

1 SMALL YELLOW ONION, CHOPPED

3 LARGE CARROTS, CHOPPED

3 GARLIC CLOVES, MINCED

1 TEASPOON GROUND CUMIN

½ TEASPOON GROUND TURMERIC

¼ TEASPOON GROUND NUTMEG

¼ TEASPOON GROUND CINNAMON

¼ TEASPOON CAYENNE PEPPER

1½ CUPS COOKED COUSCOUS

LIGHTLY TOASTED PITA BREAD, QUARTERED (OPTIONAL)

1. Combine the chickpeas, tomatoes with their juices, vegetable stock, yellow onion, carrots, garlic, cumin, turmeric, nutmeg, cinnamon, and cayenne pepper in the slow cooker and stir well.

2. Cover and cook on low for 8 to 10 hours or on high for 3 to 4 hours.

3. Add the cooked couscous during the last 15 minutes of cooking.

4. Serve hot with the pita bread, if desired.

Barley and Beans

MAKES 4 SERVINGS

Barley has similarities to pasta in terms of its consistency and to nuts in terms of its flavor. A whole grain, barley is a good source of selenium, tryptophan, copper, manganese, and phosphorus, as well as dietary fiber. Barley's fiber content has a unique relationship with cholesterol and a twofold effect in the body. The insoluble fiber in barley contains propionic acid, which works to lower cholesterol levels by inhibiting an enzyme that signals the liver to produce cholesterol. Beta glucan, another component of the fiber in barley, lowers cholesterol by ridding the body of cholesterol-containing bile acids.

3 CUPS VEGETABLE STOCK (PAGE 20)

1 (28-OUNCE) CAN FIRE-ROASTED CRUSHED TOMATOES

1 (15-OUNCE) CAN KIDNEY BEANS, RINSED AND DRAINED

1 CUP UNCOOKED BARLEY, RINSED

1 SMALL RED ONION, FINELY CHOPPED

1 CELERY STALK, CHOPPED

1 GARLIC CLOVE, MINCED

1 TEASPOON SEA SALT

¼ TEASPOON CRACKED BLACK PEPPER

¼ TEASPOON RED PEPPER FLAKES

2 BAY LEAVES

SOURDOUGH BREAD (OPTIONAL)

1. Add the vegetable stock, tomatoes, kidney beans, barley, red onion, celery, garlic, sea salt, black pepper, red pepper flakes, and bay leaves to the slow cooker. Do not stir.

2. Cover and cook on low for 7 hours.

3. Remove the bay leaves.

4. Stir and serve hot with the sourdough bread, if desired.

Beans and Molasses

Blackstrap molasses provides extra flavor as well as a nutritional boost to this bean and rice dish. Blackstrap molasses comes from the third boiling of sugar syrup and supplies almost 20 percent of your recommended daily intake of vitamin B6, as well as calcium, magnesium, iron, manganese, and potassium.

1 (15-OUNCE) CAN CHILI BEANS, UNDRAINED

1 (15-OUNCE) CAN KIDNEY BEANS, RINSED AND DRAINED

1 (14½-OUNCE) CAN DICED TOMATOES, UNDRAINED

1 LARGE YELLOW ONION, CHOPPED

1 LARGE GREEN BELL PEPPER, SEEDED AND CHOPPED

2 TABLESPOONS PACKED DARK BROWN SUGAR

2 TABLESPOONS BLACKSTRAP MOLASSES

SLOW-COOKED BROWN BASMATI RICE (PAGE 22)

1. Combine the chili beans with their juices, kidney beans, tomatoes with their juices, onion, and bell pepper in the slow cooker.

2. Stir in the sugar and blackstrap molasses.

3. Cover and cook on low for 6 to 8 hours.

4. Serve hot with the rice.

Grains with Sesame Seeds

MAKES 8 SERVINGS

There is about as much nutrition here as you can get into one bowl. The grains and fruit provide nonstop energy to keep you going all day long. This meal isn't just for breakfast, either. These anytime grains are great for dinner and will get you through to the morning feeling full and satisfied. Add a banana or whole-grain toast for even more nutrients and fiber.

NONSTICK COOKING SPRAY

½ CUP UNCOOKED BULGUR (CRACKED WHEAT)

½ CUP UNCOOKED LONG-GRAIN BROWN BASMATI RICE

½ CUP ROLLED OATS

¼ CUP UNCOOKED BARLEY

¼ CUP CORNMEAL

½ CUP PACKED LIGHT BROWN SUGAR

⅔ CUP DRIED CRANBERRIES

⅔ CUP CHOPPED DRIED APRICOTS

½ CUP DRIED CHERRIES

2 TEASPOONS GROUND CINNAMON

6 CUPS WATER

2 TABLESPOONS VANILLA EXTRACT

¼ CUP TOASTED SESAME SEEDS

1. Lightly spray the slow cooker with the nonstick cooking spray.

2. Combine the bulgur, brown rice, oats, barley, cornmeal, brown sugar, cranberries, apricots, cherries, and cinnamon in the slow cooker.

3. Add the water and vanilla and stir well.

4. Cover and cook on low for 4 to 7 hours.

5. Stir the grains before serving.

6. Sprinkle with the sesame seeds and serve hot.

Mexican Black-Eyed Peas

MAKES 8 SERVINGS

Black-eyed peas are a popular food in the South and are usually accompanied by some type of pork, greens, and, very often, freshly baked cornbread. This recipe passes on the pork, and even though it goes for a more Mexican approach, these black-eyed peas can be served with the familiar side dishes. How about a side of lightly steamed collards and some of that cornbread?

4 (15-OUNCE) CANS BLACK-EYED PEAS, RINSED AND DRAINED

1 (14½-OUNCE) CAN DICED TOMATOES, UNDRAINED

1 MEDIUM YELLOW ONION, CHOPPED

1 MEDIUM RED BELL PEPPER, SEEDED AND CHOPPED

1 CUP CHOPPED CELERY

2 TABLESPOONS PACKED LIGHT BROWN SUGAR

1 TABLESPOON CHILI POWDER

1½ TEASPOONS GARLIC SALT

SEA SALT AND CRACKED BLACK PEPPER, TO TASTE

WATER, AS NEEDED

1. Combine the black-eyed peas, tomatoes with their juices, onion, bell pepper, celery, brown sugar, chili powder, and garlic salt in the slow cooker and stir well.

2. Season with the sea salt and black pepper and stir.

3. Add water as needed.

4. Cover and cook on low for 2 hours.

5. Serve hot.

Bean Smorgasbord

MAKES 8 SERVINGS

Beans are a powerhouse of nutrients and full of health-promoting benefits. With plenty of antioxidants, dietary fiber, iron, magnesium, potassium, copper, zinc, B vitamins, and protein, beans are recommended as a part of a healthful dietary regimen. Serve with Slow-Cooked Brown Basmati Rice (page 22) and this bean smorgasbord becomes a complete meal.

1 (15-OUNCE) CAN BLACK BEANS, RINSED AND DRAINED

1 (15-OUNCE) CAN RED BEANS, RINSED AND DRAINED

1 (15-OUNCE) CAN GREAT NORTHERN BEANS, RINSED AND DRAINED

1 (15-OUNCE) CAN BLACK-EYED PEAS, RINSED AND DRAINED

1 (8½-OUNCE) CAN BABY LIMA BEANS, RINSED AND DRAINED

1½ CUPS KETCHUP

1 CUP CHOPPED YELLOW ONION

1 CUP CHOPPED GREEN BELL PEPPER

1 CUP CHOPPED RED BELL PEPPER

½ CUP PACKED LIGHT BROWN SUGAR

½ CUP WATER

2 TEASPOONS APPLE CIDER VINEGAR

1 TEASPOON MUSTARD POWDER

2 BAY LEAVES

⅛ TEASPOON CRACKED BLACK PEPPER

1. Combine the black beans, red beans, great northern beans, black-eyed peas, lima beans, ketchup, onion, and green and red bell peppers in the slow cooker.

2. Stir in the brown sugar, water, vinegar, mustard powder, bay leaves, and black pepper.

3. Cover and cook on low for 6 to 7 hours, or until the onion and bell pepper are tender.

4. Remove the bay leaves.

5. Serve hot.

Spicy Lentils

MAKES 4 SERVINGS

This dish comes with its own set of perks, in addition to lentils' beneficial properties. Research shows that spicy foods lower cholesterol, blood pressure, and inflammation. Spicy foods can even help you have a better day: serotonin, the hormone associated with feeling happy, is elevated after eating spicy foods.

1 (28-OUNCE) CAN CRUSHED TOMATOES

1 CUP CHOPPED YELLOW ONION

5 GARLIC CLOVES, MINCED

1 MEDIUM GREEN CHILE, SEEDED AND MINCED

½ CUP MEDIUM-HOT PICANTE SAUCE

¼ CUP DRIED LENTILS, RINSED

1 TEASPOON SUGAR

½ TEASPOON CUMIN SEEDS

PILAF-STYLE RICE (PAGE 23)

1. Combine the tomatoes, onion, garlic, chile, picante sauce, lentils, and sugar in the slow cooker and stir well.

2. Cover and cook on low for 6 to 8 hours, or until the lentils are tender.

3. In a small nonstick skillet, toast the cumin seeds, stirring constantly.

4. Stir the toasted cumin seeds into the stew.

5. Serve hot with the rice.

Slow-Cooked Stuffing

MAKES 8 SERVINGS

Whether you and your family call it dressing or stuffing, who doesn't love it? Usually reserved for holiday meals, slow-cooked stuffing can make stuffing a regular addition to your menu. Serve with homemade mashed potatoes, cranberry sauce, green beans, and Slow-Cooked Seitan (page 24) for that everyday special occasion known as dinner.

2 CUPS CHOPPED YELLOW ONION

2 CUPS CHOPPED CELERY

4 CUPS SLICED MUSHROOMS

¼ CUP CHOPPED PARSLEY

3½ TO 4½ CUPS VEGETABLE STOCK

12 CUPS TOASTED WHOLE-WHEAT BREAD CRUMBS

1½ TEASPOONS DRIED SAGE

1 TEASPOON DRIED THYME

1 TEASPOON POULTRY SEASONING

½ TEASPOON SEA SALT

½ TEASPOON CRACKED BLACK PEPPER

½ TEASPOON DRIED MARJORAM

1. In a large nonstick skillet, sauté the onion, celery, mushroom, and parsley in a small amount of the vegetable stock.

2. In a large bowl, combine the sautéed vegetables, bread crumbs, sage, thyme, poultry seasoning, sea salt, black pepper, and marjoram. Mix thoroughly.

3. Pour in enough vegetable stock to moisten the bread crumbs.

4. Pack the stuffing lightly into the slow cooker.

5. Cover and cook on high for 45 minutes.

6. Reduce the heat to low and cook for an additional 3 to 4 hours. If a moister stuffing is desired, add the remaining broth halfway through the cooking process.

7. Serve hot.

Lentil Pasta Sauce

MAKES 4 TO 6 SERVINGS

Angel hair pasta topped with a sauce made with lentils is a great way to get your beans in. Serve with homemade garlic bread to complete the meal in a delicious way. Choose either an Italian or French loaf. Slice in half lengthwise, then lightly cover with vegan margarine and garlic salt and toast in the oven. Perfect for dipping.

1 (14 ½-OUNCE) CAN DICED TOMATOES, UNDRAINED

1 (8-OUNCE) CAN TOMATO SAUCE

½ CUP DRIED LENTILS, RINSED

½ CUP CHOPPED YELLOW ONIONS

½ CUP CHOPPED CARROT

½ CUP CHOPPED CELERY

½ TEASPOON DRIED OREGANO

½ TEASPOON DRIED BASIL

½ TEASPOON GARLIC POWDER

¼ TEASPOON RED PEPPER FLAKES

4 CUPS FRESHLY COOKED ANGEL HAIR PASTA

1. Combine the tomatoes with their juices, tomato sauce, lentils, onions, carrots, and celery in the slow cooker.

2. Stir in the oregano, basil, garlic powder, and red pepper flakes.

3. Cover and cook on low for 8 to 10 hours or on high for 3 to 5 hours.

4. Place the pasta in a large serving bowl and pour the lentil sauce over the top.

5. Toss the pasta and lentil sauce together.

6. Serve hot.

Mac and Cheese

Homemade mac and cheese is so much better than that stuff that comes out of a box, full of questionable ingredients. This recipe for the ultimate comfort food is vegan, slow cooked, gluten-free (thanks to the quinoa pasta), and downright good, too.

2 CUPS WATER

1 CUP UNSWEETENED SOY MILK

1 (8-OUNCE) PACKAGE QUINOA ELBOW MACARONI

3 CUPS CHOPPED BROCCOLI FLORETS

⅔ CUP NUTRITIONAL YEAST

½ CUP VEGAN CREAM CHEESE, SOFTENED

3 TABLESPOONS VEGAN MARGARINE, SOFTENED

2 TABLESPOONS TAHINI

1½ TEASPOONS SEA SALT

1 TEASPOON MUSTARD POWDER

½ TEASPOON PAPRIKA

¼ TEASPOON CAYENNE PEPPER

¼ TEASPOON GROUND TURMERIC

1. Combine 1½ cups of the water, the soy milk, macaroni, broccoli, nutritional yeast, vegan cream cheese, vegan margarine, and tahini in the slow cooker.

2. Stir in the sea salt, mustard powder, paprika, cayenne pepper, and turmeric.

3. Cover and cook on low for 1 hour.

4. Stir in the remaining ½ cup water.

5. Cover and cook an additional 30 to 45 minutes, or until the pasta is done.

6. Serve hot.

Macaroni Casserole Florentine

MAKES 4 SERVINGS

"Florentine" was once used to describe the cooking style of Florence, in Italy, but now means any dish prepared with spinach. This macaroni casserole is actually a faux mac and cheese of sorts. The raw cashews help give it its cheesy consistency and rich flavor. This dish is delicious served with a side of stewed tomatoes.

NONSTICK COOKING SPRAY

1 (8-OUNCE) PACKAGE ELBOW MACARONI, COOKED AL DENTE

1 (10-OUNCE) PACKAGE FROZEN CHOPPED SPINACH, THAWED
   AND DRAINED

2 TABLESPOONS OLIVE OIL

1 MEDIUM YELLOW ONION, CHOPPED

½ CUP RAW CASHEWS

1¾ CUPS WATER

1 (15-OUNCE) CAN WHITE BEANS, RINSED AND DRAINED

1 TABLESPOON WHITE MISO PASTE

2 TEASPOONS FRESH LEMON JUICE

¼ TEASPOON MUSTARD POWDER

¼ TEASPOON CAYENNE PEPPER

PINCH OF GROUND NUTMEG

SEA SALT, TO TASTE

½ CUP TOASTED DRY BREAD CRUMBS

1. Lightly spray the slow cooker with the nonstick cooking spray.

2. In a large bowl, combine the cooked macaroni and the spinach. Set aside.

3. In a small nonstick skillet, heat 1 tablespoon of the olive oil over medium heat.

continued ▶

4. Add the onion to the skillet and cook until softened, about 5 minutes. Set aside.

5. Grind the cashews into a powder in a blender or food processor.

6. Add 1 cup of the water to the cashews and blend or process until smooth.

7. Add the softened onion, white beans, miso paste, remaining ¾ cup of water, lemon juice, mustard powder, cayenne pepper, nutmeg, and sea salt to the cashew mixture in the blender or food processor.

8. Blend or process all the ingredients until smooth.

9. Pour the cashew mixture over the elbow macaroni and the spinach and mix thoroughly.

10. Transfer the cashew and spinach mixture to the slow cooker.

11. Cover and cook on low for 3 hours.

12. Sprinkle the toasted bread crumbs over the casserole and serve hot.

Vegan Risotto

MAKES 4 TO 6 SERVINGS

There is rice and then there is risotto. Risotto is a rice dish from Italy that is characterized by its creamy sauce. A stickier rice makes the creamiest risotto, so Arborio rice is called for in this recipe. Risotto is often served as a side dish with veal shanks, but this version can be served with Slow-Cooked Black Beans (page 26) or canned beans.

1 TABLESPOON OLIVE OIL

1 MEDIUM YELLOW ONION, CHOPPED

4 CUPS VEGETABLE STOCK (PAGE 20)

¾ CUP UNCOOKED ARBORIO RICE

1 MEDIUM ACORN SQUASH, PEELED AND DICED

1 LARGE CARROT, DICED

1 TEASPOON CRACKED BLACK PEPPER

1. In a small nonstick skillet heat the olive oil over medium heat.

2. Add the onion and sauté until brown and caramelized.

3. Combine the vegetable stock, rice, squash, carrot, and black pepper in the slow cooker.

4. Stir in the caramelized onion.

5. Cover and cook on high for 3 to 4 hours.

6. Serve hot.

Spaghetti and Hot Dogs

MAKES 6 SERVINGS

Spaghetti and hot dogs make a great kid-friendly vegan meal. The spaghetti supplies the grain and the hot dogs supply the fun.

NONSTICK COOKING SPRAY

2 CUPS UNCOOKED BROKEN SPAGHETTI

1 (16-OUNCE) PACKAGE VEGAN HOT DOGS, CUT INTO ½-INCH PIECES

1½ CUPS DICED ZUCCHINI

1 CUP SHREDDED CARROTS

2 CUPS HOT WATER

1 (8-OUNCE) CAN TOMATO SAUCE

2 TEASPOONS SWEETENER OF YOUR CHOICE

1½ TEASPOONS ITALIAN SEASONING

CRUSTY GARLIC BREAD (OPTIONAL)

1. Generously spray the slow cooker with the nonstick cooking spray.

2. Combine the spaghetti, vegan hot dogs, zucchini, and carrots in the slow cooker.

3. In a medium bowl, combine the water, tomato sauce, sweetener, and Italian seasoning.

4. Pour the tomato sauce mixture over the spaghetti mixture in the slow cooker.

5. Cover and cook on low for 4 to 6 hours.

6. Mix well before serving.

7. Serve hot with the crusty garlic bread, if desired.

Southern-Style Casserole

MAKES 4 TO 6 SERVINGS

Beans and cornbread are Southern classics. Starting in 1981, beans and cornbread were the traditional meal at NASA after a shuttle launch, and they became a symbol of success for the space program. This Southern-Style Casserole is a slow-cooked variation of beans and cornbread, and can be enjoyed not only in the South but wherever good food is appreciated.

NONSTICK COOKING SPRAY

1 LARGE RED BELL PEPPER, SEEDED AND CHOPPED

1 LARGE WHITE ONION, CHOPPED

3 GARLIC CLOVES, MINCED

1 (15-OUNCE) CAN RED KIDNEY BEANS, RINSED AND DRAINED

1 (15-OUNCE) CAN PINTO BEANS, RINSED AND DRAINED

1 (15-OUNCE) CAN BLACK BEANS, RINSED AND DRAINED

1 (14½-OUNCE) CAN DICED TOMATOES WITH CHILES, UNDRAINED

1 (8-OUNCE) CAN TOMATO SAUCE

1 (8-OUNCE) CAN CREAMED CORN

3 TEASPOONS SEA SALT

2 TEASPOONS CHILI POWDER

1 TEASPOON CRACKED BLACK PEPPER

1 TEASPOON HOT SAUCE

¾ CUP SOY MILK

½ CUP YELLOW CORNMEAL

½ CUP ALL-PURPOSE FLOUR

1½ TABLESPOONS VEGETABLE OIL

1 TABLESPOON SUGAR

1¼ TEASPOONS BAKING POWDER

EGG SUBSTITUTE FOR 1 EGG

1. Lightly spray the slow cooker with the nonstick cooking spray.

2. In a nonstick skillet over medium heat, sauté the bell pepper, onion, and garlic in a small amount of water until tender.

continued ▶

3. Add the sautéed vegetables to the slow cooker.

4. Combine the red kidney beans, pinto beans, black beans, tomatoes with their juices, tomato sauce, half of the creamed corn, 2 teaspoons of the sea salt, the chili powder, black pepper, and hot sauce in the slow cooker and stir well.

5. Cover and cook on high for 1 hour.

6. In a large bowl, combine the soy milk, cornmeal, flour, vegetable oil, sugar, baking powder, egg substitute, remaining 1 teaspoon sea salt, and remaining creamed corn and mix thoroughly.

7. Add the soy milk mixture to the slow cooker and completely cover the top of the bean mixture. Do not stir.

8. Cover and cook for an additional 1½ to 2 hours.

9. Cook until a toothpick inserted into the center of the cornbread comes out clean.

10. Serve hot.

Lima Bean Gumbo

MAKES 8 TO 10 SERVINGS

Eighteenth-century southern Louisiana is the home of gumbo, a dish containing meat or shellfish, some type of thickener, and vegetables. Okra is the thickener of choice in this vegan gumbo that makes no apologies for the absence of meat.

2 LARGE YELLOW ONIONS, CHOPPED

2 LARGE GREEN BELL PEPPERS, SEEDED AND DICED

6 WHOLE CLOVES

8 CUPS VEGETABLE STOCK (PAGE 20)

4 CUPS DICED TOMATOES

3 CUPS SLICED OKRA

2 CUPS FROZEN CORN

2 CUPS COOKED OR CANNED LIMA BEANS

2 TEASPOONS SEA SALT

½ TEASPOON GROUND ALLSPICE

ARBORIO RICE (PAGE 23)

1. In a large nonstick skillet over medium heat, sauté the onions, bell peppers, and cloves in a small amount of water until the vegetables are soft.

2. Remove the cloves from the skillet.

3. Combine the skillet mixture, vegetable stock, tomatoes, okra, corn, lima beans, sea salt, and allspice in the slow cooker and stir well.

4. Cover and cook on low for 8 to 10 hours or on high for 6 hours.

5. Serve hot over the Arborio rice.

CHAPTER EIGHT

Vegetables

GREENS, GREENS, GREENS

ITALIAN ROASTED VEGGIES

APPLES AND CABBAGE

EGGPLANT AND CAPERS

RATATOUILLE NIÇOISE

ROOT VEGETABLES AND
    DRIED FRUIT

"CHEESY" ZUCCHINI, LEEKS,
    AND TOMATOES

CLASSIC VEGGIES AND RICE

ITALIAN OYSTER MUSHROOMS
    AND PILAF

KIDNEY BEAN AND BARLEY
    STUFFED SQUASH

"CHEESY" CAULIFLOWER

RUTABAGA AND CABBAGE STEW

EGGPLANT, OKRA, AND
    BUTTERNUT SQUASH STEW

POLENTA AND BEAN CASSEROLE

CARROT AND GREEN
    BEAN CASSEROLE

PORTOBELLO MUSHROOM
    SUBMARINE SANDWICHES

EGGPLANT PARMESAN

VEGGIE BAKE

FETTUCINE AND VEGATABLES

Vegetables

Greens, Greens, Greens

MAKES 2 SERVINGS

Greens and beans can be an entire meal by itself. Kale and collard greens are ranked as two of the most nutrient-dense foods you can eat and are probably the tastiest greens to work with. This meal can serve two; however, one hungry vegan can empty the slow cooker if you're not paying attention. Plan accordingly.

2 TABLESPOONS OLIVE OIL

½ SMALL RED ONION, DICED

2 GARLIC CLOVES, MINCED

1 (15-OUNCE) CAN BLACK BEANS, RINSED AND DRAINED

2 CUPS STEMMED, CHOPPED KALE

2 CUPS STEMMED, CHOPPED COLLARD GREENS

2 TEASPOONS HERBES DE PROVENCE

2 TABLESPOONS MISO DISSOLVED IN 1 CUP VEGETABLE STOCK (PAGE 20)

¼ TEASPOON GROUND WHITE PEPPER

1 HANDFUL CHOPPED FRESH PARSLEY

WHOLE-GRAIN BREAD (OPTIONAL)

1. Turn the slow cooker on high.

2. Add the oil, onion, and garlic.

3. Stir the ingredients in the slow cooker to coat the onions and garlic.

4. Cover and cook for 5 minutes.

5. Add the beans, kale, and collard greens.

6. Stir in the herbs de Provence, miso mixture, white pepper, and parsley.

7. Cover and cook for 1 hour.

8. Turn the slow cooker to low and cook for an additional 2 hours.

9. Serve hot with whole-grain bread, if desired.

Italian Roasted Veggies

MAKES 4 SERVINGS

Vegetables provide a lot of diversity in terms of how they can be prepared. Something as simple as a packet of Italian seasoning can make a dramatic difference in flavor. In the case of these Italian Roasted Veggies, tangy is the flavor that comes to mind. Serve a green salad alongside.

NONSTICK COOKING SPRAY

4 LARGE RED POTATOES, CUT INTO CHUNKS

2 LARGE CARROTS, SLICED

2 LARGE ZUCCHINI, THICKLY SLICED

½ LARGE RED ONION, SLICED

OLIVE OIL, FOR DRIZZLING

1 ENVELOPE DRY ITALIAN DRESSING/SEASONING MIX

1. Lightly spray the slow cooker with the nonstick cooking spray.

2. Combine the potatoes, carrots, zucchini, and onion in the slow cooker.

3. Drizzle the vegetables with the olive oil.

4. Sprinkle the dry Italian seasoning mix over the vegetables.

5. Lightly toss the vegetables to coat them with the oil and seasoning.

6. Cover and cook on low for 5 to 7 hours or on high for 3 to 4 hours.

7. Serve hot.

Apples and Cabbage

Looking for a low-calorie meal that is pleasing to the palate as well as to the waistline? How about one that is also beneficial to your health? Try Apples and Cabbage. Apples contain about 95 calories each, and cabbage just 25 calories per 100 grams. Both are rich in phytonutrients and antioxidants.

NONSTICK COOKING SPRAY
2 LARGE TART APPLES, CORED AND DICED
1 MEDIUM CABBAGE, COARSELY CHOPPED
2 MEDIUM WHITE ONIONS, QUARTERED AND SLICED
1 TEASPOON SEA SALT
¼ TEASPOON CRACKED BLACK PEPPER
1 CUP FROZEN APPLE JUICE CONCENTRATE, THAWED
½ CUP VEGETABLE STOCK (PAGE 20)
3 TABLESPOONS SPICY MUSTARD

1. Lightly spray the slow cooker with the nonstick cooking spray.

2. Combine the apples, cabbage, and onions in the slow cooker.

3. Season with the sea salt and black pepper and stir.

4. In a small bowl, combine the apple juice concentrate, vegetable stock, and mustard.

5. Pour the apple juice mixture over the cabbage mixture in the slow cooker.

6. Cover and cook on low for 6 to 8 hours, or until the vegetables are tender, stirring every 2 to 3 hours.

7. Serve hot.

Eggplant and Capers

MAKES 4 TO 6 SERVINGS

Capers are the flower buds of Capparis spinosa, *a prickly perennial plant found in the Mediterranean and certain parts of Asia. The capers and green olives that top off this dish complement each other and impart a sharp, salty flavor to other foods. Eggplant and Capers can be served as an appetizer on sliced Italian bread or as a meal served over pasta.*

2 PLUM TOMATOES, SEEDED AND CHOPPED

1 SMALL EGGPLANT, CUT INTO ½-INCH DICE

1 MEDIUM ZUCCHINI, CUT INTO ½-INCH DICE

1 CELERY STALK, CHOPPED

1 SMALL YELLOW ONION, CHOPPED

¾ CUP TOMATO PURÉE

3 TABLESPOONS RED WINE VINEGAR

1 TABLESPOON SUGAR

1 TABLESPOON DRIED PARSLEY

1½ TEASPOONS DRIED BASIL

⅓ CUP CHOPPED GREEN OLIVES

1 TABLESPOON CAPERS, DRAINED AND RINSED

1. Combine the tomatoes, eggplant, zucchini, celery, and onion in the slow cooker.

2. Stir in the tomato purée, red wine vinegar, sugar, parsley, and basil.

3. Cover and cook on low for 6 hours or on high for 4 hours.

4. Stir in the olives and capers.

5. Serve warm or at room temperature, or chill overnight.

Ratatouille Niçoise

MAKES 6 SERVINGS

Ratatouille Niçoise is a stewed vegetable dish with its roots in Nice, France. There are many approaches to preparing this dish, but the best option is the slow cooker, since the long simmering enhances the flavors. For a complete meal, serve with a loaf of warm French bread and a little olive oil for dipping.

1 (14½-OUNCE) CAN CRUSHED TOMATOES

1 CUP VEGETABLE STOCK (PAGE 20)

1 POUND EGGPLANT, PEELED AND CUT INTO CUBES

2 LARGE ZUCCHINI, PEELED, HALVED, AND THINLY SLICED

1 LARGE YELLOW CROOKNECK SQUASH, PEELED, HALVED,
    AND THINLY SLICED

1 MEDIUM YELLOW ONION, SLICED

1 MEDIUM RED BELL PEPPER, SEEDED AND THINLY SLICED

2 GARLIC CLOVES, MINCED

JUICE AND ZEST OF 1 LARGE LEMON

1 TEASPOON DRIED OREGANO

SEA SALT AND CRACKED BLACK PEPPER, TO TASTE

CHOPPED FRESH BASIL (OPTIONAL)

OLIVE OIL (OPTIONAL)

CRUMBLED VEGAN FETA CHEESE (OPTIONAL)

1. Combine the crushed tomatoes, vegetable stock, eggplant, zucchini, squash, onion, bell pepper, and garlic in the slow cooker.

2. Stir in the lemon juice, lemon zest, oregano, sea salt, and black pepper.

3. Cover and cook on low for 6 to 8 hours or on high for 4 to 6 hours.

4. Serve hot, garnished with the fresh basil, a drizzle of olive oil, and the vegan feta cheese, if desired.

Root Vegetables and Dried Fruit

Root vegetables are earthy and grounding and provide healthful sugars and carbohydrates. Dried fruit provides the body with carbohydrates, too, and a little more sugar than root vegetables or regular fruit. The drying process causes the sugar to become more concentrated and even sweeter.

1 POUND PARSNIPS, PEELED AND DICED

1 POUND TURNIPS, PEELED AND DICED

1 POUND CARROTS, PEELED AND DICED

2 MEDIUM YELLOW ONIONS, CHOPPED

6 DRIED APRICOTS, CHOPPED

4 PITTED PRUNES, CHOPPED

1 TABLESPOON DRIED PARSLEY

1 TABLESPOON DRIED CILANTRO

1 TEASPOON GROUND TURMERIC

1 TEASPOON GROUND CUMIN

½ TEASPOON GROUND GINGER

½ TEASPOON GROUND CINNAMON

¼ TEASPOON CAYENNE PEPPER

1¾ CUPS VEGETABLE STOCK (PAGE 20)

ARBORIO RICE (PAGE 23) (OPTIONAL)

1. Combine the parsnips, turnips, carrots, onions, apricots, and prunes in the slow cooker.

2. Add the parsley, cilantro, turmeric, cumin, ginger, cinnamon, and cayenne pepper.

3. Pour in the vegetable stock and stir.

4. Cover and cook on low for 9 hours.

5. Serve hot with the Arborio rice, if desired.

"Cheesy" Zucchini, Leeks, and Tomatoes

MAKES 6 SERVINGS

Depending on how hungry you are, these "cheesy" veggies plus some garlic bread can make a meal, or try them on top of pasta, noodles, or rice.

4 TABLESPOONS OLIVE OIL

2 LEEKS, SLICED

½ CUP VEGETABLE STOCK (PAGE 20)

2 TABLESPOONS TOMATO PASTE

2 TEASPOONS DRIED TARRAGON

3 MEDIUM TOMATOES, SLICED AND LIBERALLY SALTED

4 CUPS SHREDDED ZUCCHINI, SALTED AND DRAINED

4 OUNCES GRATED VEGAN PARMESAN CHEESE

GARLIC BREAD (OPTIONAL)

1. Add 2 tablespoons olive oil to the bottom of the slow cooker.

2. In a medium bowl, toss the leeks with the remaining 2 tablespoons olive oil. Set aside.

3. In a small bowl, combine the vegetable stock, tomato paste, and tarragon and mix well. Set aside.

4. Layer the bottom of the slow cooker with a portion of the sliced tomatoes.

5. Sprinkle the tomatoes with a portion of the tomato paste mixture.

6. Add a layer of zucchini, a layer of cheese, and another layer of the tomato paste mixture.

7. Add a portion of the leeks.

8. Continue the layering process, ending with the tomato paste, until the pot is three-quarters full or there are no ingredients remaining.

continued ▶

9. Cover and cook on high for 2 hours, or until the vegetables are tender.

10. Uncover and cook on low for 1 additional hour.

11. Serve hot with garlic bread, if desired.

Classic Veggies and Rice

MAKES 6 TO 8 SERVINGS

Just like beans and rice, veggies and rice are a vegan staple. This selection of vegetables offers a nutrient-dense approach to eating, and when combined with the rice is very satisfying. Want different vegetables? Any will do. Serve this classic dish with a large green salad and whole-grain bread for a perfect meal.

2 (14½-OUNCE) CANS DICED TOMATOES, UNDRAINED

1 CUP WATER

2 MEDIUM YELLOW ONIONS, CHOPPED

2 MEDIUM CARROTS, THINLY SLICED

1 LARGE POTATO, PEELED AND CUT INTO 1-INCH CUBES

¾ CUP UNCOOKED CONVERTED LONG-GRAIN RICE

½ CUP OLIVE OIL

2 TABLESPOONS FRESH LEMON JUICE

1 CUP FROZEN PEAS

2 TABLESPOONS CHOPPED FRESH PARSLEY

1 TABLESPOON SEA SALT

2 ZUCCHINI, CHOPPED

1 LARGE GREEN BELL PEPPER, SEEDED AND CHOPPED

1. Combine 1 can of tomatoes with their juices, ½ cup of the water, the onions, carrots, potato, rice, olive oil, and lemon juice in the slow cooker and stir well.

2. Cover and cook on high for 1 hour.

3. Stir in the remaining 1 can of tomatoes with their juices, remaining ½ cup of water, peas, parsley, sea salt, zucchini, and bell pepper.

4. Cover and cook for an additional 30 to 60 minutes, or until the vegetables are tender but not mushy.

5. Serve hot.

Italian Oyster Mushrooms and Pilaf

MAKES 4 TO 5 SERVINGS

Oyster mushrooms, and all mushrooms for that matter, are technically not vegetables; they are fungi. Oyster mushrooms supply good amounts of iron, potassium, and protein. And even though most vegans don't need to be concerned about lowering their cholesterol, these mushrooms contain a naturally occurring substance called lovastatin that can do just that.

1 TABLESPOON OLIVE OIL

3 LARGE RED BELL PEPPERS, SEEDED AND CHOPPED

3 LARGE GREEN BELL PEPPERS, SEEDED AND CHOPPED

2 LARGE YELLOW ONIONS, CHOPPED

12 OUNCES OYSTER MUSHROOMS, CHOPPED

4 GARLIC CLOVES, MINCED

1 (28-OUNCE) CAN CRUSHED TOMATOES

10 FRESH BASIL LEAVES, CHOPPED

1 TABLESPOON SEA SALT

1½ TEASPOONS CRACKED BLACK PEPPER

3 BAY LEAVES

PILAF-STYLE RICE (PAGE 23)

1. In a large nonstick skillet, heat the olive oil over medium heat.

2. Sauté the red and green bell peppers and onions until soft.

3. Stir in the mushrooms and garlic and sauté just until the mushrooms begin to brown.

4. Transfer the contents of the skillet to the slow cooker.

5. Stir in the tomatoes, basil, sea salt, black pepper, and bay leaves.

6. Cover and cook on low for 6 to 8 hours.

7. Remove the bay leaves.

8. Serve hot with the rice.

Kidney Bean and Barley Stuffed Squash

MAKES 4 SERVINGS

The carnival squash is the highlight of this dish. Somewhat similar in taste to sweet potatoes and butternut squash, the carnival squash has a unique flavor all its own. Resembling a small pumpkin, the carnival squash is the offspring of the sweet dumpling squash and the acorn squash. Like most squash, carnival squash is abundant in carotenoids and vitamins A and C. Serve with lightly steamed greens for a complete meal.

1 CUP COOKED BARLEY

1 CUP COOKED OR CANNED KIDNEY BEANS, RINSED AND DRAINED

¼ CUP MINCED YELLOW ONION

2 GARLIC CLOVES, MINCED

2 TABLESPOONS ROASTED SUNFLOWER SEEDS

1½ TABLESPOONS TAMARI

¾ TEASPOON DRIED OREGANO

¾ TEASPOON DRIED BASIL

½ TEASPOON GROUND CUMIN

⅛ TEASPOON CAYENNE PEPPER

2 LARGE CARNIVAL SQUASH, HALVED LENGTHWISE AND SEEDED

½ CUP VEGETABLE STOCK (PAGE 20)

1. In a medium bowl, combine the barley, beans, onion, garlic, sunflower seeds, tamari, oregano, basil, cumin, and cayenne pepper and mix well.

2. Stuff each piece of squash with one-quarter of the mixture.

3. Arrange the squash in the slow cooker.

4. Pour the vegetable stock into the bottom of the slow cooker but not on the squash.

5. Cover and cook on low for 2 to 3 hours, or until the squash is tender.

6. Serve hot.

"Cheesy" Cauliflower

MAKES 10 SERVINGS

"Cheesy" Cauliflower is a great way to increase your intake of cauliflower. Cauliflower is a cruciferous vegetable, and like all cruciferous vegetables (Brussels sprouts, kale, cabbage, bok choy, and broccoli) should be eaten at least 2 or 3 times a week. Research shows the phytochemicals in cruciferous vegetables, specifically sulforaphane, can stop cancer before it even starts by activating enzymes that "disable" carcinogens before they can do any harm.

NONSTICK COOKING SPRAY

3 CUPS COOKED RICE

2 CUPS SHREDDED VEGAN CHEDDAR CHEESE

1 (14½-OUNCE) CAN VEGAN CREAM OF MUSHROOM SOUP

1 HEAD CAULIFLOWER, CUT INTO FLORETS

1 MEDIUM YELLOW ONION, DICED

8 OUNCES WHITE MUSHROOMS, SLICED

½ CUP WATER

1. Lightly spray the slow cooker with the nonstick cooking spray.

2. Combine the rice, vegan cheddar cheese, mushroom soup, cauliflower, onion, mushrooms, and water in the slow cooker and stir well.

3. Cover and cook on low for 4 to 6 hours.

4. Serve hot

Rutabaga and Cabbage Stew

MAKES 6 TO 8 SERVINGS

Rutabaga, also known as yellow turnip or Swedish turnip, is a cross between a turnip and a cabbage. Rutabaga, a root vegetable, is paired with cabbage, chickpeas, and barley in this stew to bring you a hearty meal.

1 (2-INCH) PIECE DRIED KOMBU SEAWEED

1 LARGE YELLOW ONION, CHOPPED

1 CELERY STALK, SLICED

2 LARGE CARROTS, THINLY SLICED

2 GARLIC CLOVES, MINCED

6 CUPS VEGETABLE STOCK (PAGE 20)

1 (15-OUNCE) CAN CHICKPEAS, RINSED AND DRAINED

¾ CUP QUICK-COOKING BARLEY

1 MEDIUM RUTABAGA, PEELED AND FINELY DICED

½ GREEN CABBAGE, SLICED INTO THIN RIBBONS

2 TABLESPOONS TAMARI

1 TABLESPOON APPLE CIDER VINEGAR

½ TEASPOON SEA SALT

½ TEASPOON CRACKED BLACK PEPPER

½ TEASPOON DRIED TARRAGON

FRESH BISCUITS (OPTIONAL)

1. In a small bowl, soak the kombu for 10 minutes with just enough water to cover.

2. Combine the onion, celery, carrots, and garlic in the slow cooker.

3. Pour in the vegetable stock.

4. Stir in the chickpeas, barley, rutabaga, cabbage, tamari, apple cider vinegar, sea salt, black pepper, and tarragon.

5. Dice the softened kombu.

continued ▶

6. Add the kombu and its soaking water to the slow cooker.

7. Cover and cook on low for 6 to 7 hours or on high for 4 hours, or until the vegetables and the barley are tender.

8. Ladle the stew into bowls and serve hot with fresh biscuits, if desired.

Eggplant, Okra, and Butternut Squash Stew

MAKES 10 SERVINGS

Okra is one of the most nutritious veggies out there. Okra comes in a pod and brings with it not only an interesting flavor but an array of nutrients, too. One of the most important nutrients okra provides is folate. Folate is needed to absorb B12, which is necessary to keep homocysteine, a well-known marker for heart disease, down to a healthful level.

1 BUTTERNUT SQUASH, PEELED, SEEDED, AND CUT INTO 1-INCH CUBES

1 LARGE CARROT, SLICED

2 CUPS 1-INCH CUBES EGGPLANT

2 CUPS 1-INCH CUBES ZUCCHINI

1 (10-OUNCE) PACKAGE FROZEN OKRA, THAWED

1 (8-OUNCE) CAN TOMATO SAUCE

½ CUP VEGETABLE STOCK (PAGE 20)

⅓ CUP RAISINS

1 MEDIUM YELLOW ONION, CHOPPED

1 GARLIC CLOVE, CHOPPED

½ TEASPOON GROUND CUMIN

½ TEASPOON GROUND TURMERIC

¼ TEASPOON RED PEPPER FLAKES

¼ TEASPOON GROUND CINNAMON

¼ TEASPOON GROUND PAPRIKA

SLOW-COOKED BROWN BASMATI RICE (PAGE 22) (OPTIONAL)

1. Combine the butternut squash, carrot, eggplant, zucchini, okra, tomato sauce, vegetable stock, and raisins in the slow cooker.

2. Stir in the onion, garlic, cumin, turmeric, red pepper flakes, cinnamon, and paprika.

3. Cover and cook on low for 7 to 9 hours.

4. Ladle the stew into bowls and serve hot with the rice, if desired.

Polenta and Bean Casserole

Modern-day polenta is made from cornmeal that has been boiled with water into a porridge-like consistency. Polenta is most often sold as a small refrigerated tube that can be sliced and then baked, fried, grilled, or slow-cooked. Polenta supplies almost 10 grams of protein per 8-ounce serving. It's classified as a grain, but many consider corn (and polenta) to be a vegetable.

2 (15-OUNCE) CANS CANNELLINI BEANS, RINSED AND DRAINED

1 (15-OUNCE) CAN CHICKPEAS, RINSED AND DRAINED

1 MEDIUM YELLOW ONION, CHOPPED

4 GARLIC CLOVES, MINCED

¼ CUP VEGAN BASIL PESTO

1½ TEASPOONS DRIED ITALIAN SEASONING

1 (16-OUNCE) PACKAGE COOKED PLAIN POLENTA, CUT INTO
   ½-INCH SLICES

4 OUNCES SHREDDED VEGAN MOZZARELLA CHEESE

4 OUNCES GRATED VEGAN PARMESAN CHEESE

2 CUPS FRESH SPINACH (BABY SPINACH OR LARGER LEAVES, TORN)

1 CUP TORN RADICCHIO

1 LARGE TOMATO, THINLY SLICED

1 TABLESPOON WATER

1. In a large bowl, combine the beans, chickpeas, onion, garlic, half of the basil pesto, and Italian seasoning and stir well.

2. Layer the bottom of the slow cooker with half of the bean mixture, half of the polenta, half of the vegan mozzarella cheese, and half of the vegan Parmesan cheese.

3. Add the remaining bean mixture and the remaining polenta to the slow cooker.

4. Cover and cook on low for 4 to 6 hours or on high for 2 to 2½ hours.

5. Add the spinach, radicchio, tomato, remaining vegan mozzarella cheese, and remaining vegan Parmesan cheese to the slow cooker.

6. Combine the remaining pesto and 1 tablespoon water.

7. Drizzle the pesto mixture over the casserole.

8. Leave uncovered for 5 minutes.

9. Serve hot.

Carrot and Green Bean Casserole

MAKES 4 TO 6 SERVINGS

What do carrots and green beans have in common? Besides being healthful and tasty, they contain the same type of carotenoids, beta carotene and lutein. Green beans are just better at hiding their carotenoid content than carrots due to the green bean's concentration of chlorophyll. This casserole goes great with a baked potato on the side.

2 (14½-OUNCE) CANS GREEN BEANS, DRAINED

2 CUPS THINLY SLICED CARROTS

2 CUPS THINLY SLICED CELERY

½ CUP CHOPPED WHITE ONION

¼ CUP DICED GREEN BELL PEPPER

2 CUPS TOMATO JUICE

3 TABLESPOONS QUICK-COOKING TAPIOCA

1 TABLESPOON SUGAR

1 TEASPOON SEA SALT

CRACKED BLACK PEPPER, TO TASTE

2 TABLESPOONS VEGAN MARGARINE, CUT INTO BITS

TOASTED BREAD CRUMBS

1. Combine the green beans, carrots, celery, onion, bell pepper, tomato juice, tapioca, sugar, sea salt, and black pepper in the slow cooker and stir well.

2. Scatter the bits of vegan margarine over the top of the ingredients in the slow cooker.

3. Cover and cook on low for 7 to 9 hours or on high for 3½ to 4½ hours.

4. Sprinkle the toasted bread crumbs over the top of the casserole.

5. Serve hot.

Portobello Mushroom Submarine Sandwiches

You can make sandwiches in the slow cooker? No, but you can make sandwich fixings. The portabello mushroom (the vegan's answer to meat) takes center stage in this tangy approach to a submarine sandwich. Serve with a few baked potato chips and lunch is on.

4 LARGE PORTABELLO MUSHROOMS, STEMS REMOVED AND CAPS SLICED
1 (7-OUNCE) JAR ROASTED RED PEPPERS, DRAINED
¼ CUP PREPARED ITALIAN DRESSING
4 SUBMARINE ROLLS

1. Combine the mushrooms and the roasted peppers in the slow cooker.

2. Pour in the Italian dressing and stir.

3. Cover and cook on low for 4 to 5 hours or on high for 2 hours.

4. Assemble sandwiches by dividing the mushrooms and peppers among the rolls.

Eggplant Parmesan

MAKES 4 TO 6 SERVINGS

Eggplant Parmesan is a favorite among vegetarians. Vegans usually have to pass on this scrumptious dish because of the egg in the breading and the cheese on top, but not in this case. Serve with your favorite pasta and bread and remember how good Eggplant Parmesan can be. This one takes a little more space and will do better in a larger slow cooker.

NONSTICK COOKING SPRAY

2 (25-OUNCE) JARS PASTA SAUCE

1 LARGE EGGPLANT, PEELED AND THINLY SLICED

3 CUPS SHREDDED VEGAN MOZZARELLA CHEESE

¾ CUP GRATED VEGAN PARMESAN CHEESE

ITALIAN BREAD CRUMBS, TO TASTE

1. Lightly spray the slow cooker with the nonstick cooking spray.

2. Cover the bottom of the slow cooker with half of the pasta sauce.

3. Layer some of the eggplant on top of the sauce.

4. Cover the eggplant with some of the vegan mozzarella cheese.

5. Sprinkle some of the vegan Parmesan cheese on top of the vegan mozzarella cheese.

6. Repeat the eggplant-cheese layering process three more times, finishing with the sauce and the vegan cheese.

7. Top the layers with the bread crumbs.

8. Cover and cook on low for 8 hours or on high for 5 to 6 hours.

9. Serve hot.

Veggie Bake

Creamed corn is made by a process that pulps the corn kernels and then gathers the milky residue, and sometimes contains added milk. This veggie bake passes on the milk but steps it up a notch by adding other veggies.

2 (15-OUNCE) CANS CREAMED CORN

2 (15-OUNCE) CANS CUT GREEN BEANS, DRAINED

1 (15-OUNCE) CAN PEAS, DRAINED

1 (14½-OUNCE) CAN DICED TOMATOES, DRAINED

½ CUP VEGAN MAYONNAISE

1 TEASPOON DRIED TARRAGON

1 TEASPOON DRIED BASIL

½ TEASPOON SEA SALT

CRACKED BLACK PEPPER, TO TASTE

VEGAN CORNBREAD

1. Combine the corn, green beans, peas, tomatoes, and vegan mayonnaise in the slow cooker.

2. Stir in the tarragon, basil, sea salt, and black pepper.

3. Cover and cook on low for 3 to 5 hours.

4. Serve hot with the cornbread.

Fettuccine and Vegetables

MAKES 6 SERVINGS

Pretty close to fettuccine Alfredo, Fettuccine and Vegetables is a creamy, cheesy, and delicious meal. The coconut milk replaces the dairy, and vegan cheese comes to the rescue, too. Serve like any other pasta dish and find some good bread to go with it.

2 TABLESPOONS VEGAN MARGARINE, SOFTENED

1½ CUPS FROZEN BROCCOLI FLORETS, THAWED

8 OUNCES WHITE MUSHROOMS, SLICED

2 MEDIUM CARROTS, THINLY SLICED

1 MEDIUM ZUCCHINI, THINLY SLICED

1 MEDIUM YELLOW SUMMER SQUASH, THINLY SLICED

6 SMALL SCALLIONS, SLICED

3 GARLIC CLOVES, MINCED

1 CUP GRATED VEGAN PARMESAN CHEESE

½ TEASPOON DRIED BASIL

½ TEASPOON CRACKED BLACK PEPPER

¼ TEASPOON SEA SALT

12 OUNCES FETTUCCINE, COOKED

1 CUP SHREDDED VEGAN MOZZARELLA CHEESE

½ TO 1 CUP CANNED COCONUT MILK

1. Coat the bottom of the slow cooker with the vegan margarine.

2. Combine the broccoli, mushrooms, carrots, zucchini, squash, scallions, garlic, and vegan Parmesan cheese in the slow cooker.

3. Stir in the basil, black pepper, and sea salt.

4. Cover and cook on high for 2 to 3 hours, or until vegetables are just tender.

5. Add the fettuccine, vegan mozzarella cheese, and the desired amount of coconut milk to the slow cooker and stir.

6. Cover and cook for an additional 30 minutes.

7. Serve hot.

Meat Alternatives

CRUCIFEROUS VEGETABLES, TOFU, AND RICE

CRISPY TOFU AND BROWN BASMATI RICE

BARBECUE-STYLE TOFU AND PINEAPPLE

TOFU SLOPPY JOES

TOFU AND SPINACH LASAGNA

TEMPEH WITH ALMOND BUTTER

PEANUT, TEMPEH, AND BUTTERNUT SQUASH MOLE

TEMPEH ENCHILADA CASSEROLE

PORTOBELLO MUSHROOM AND TEMPEH STROGANOFF

TEMPEH AND TOFU HUNGARIAN GOULASH

CHUNKY SEITAN ROAST

MEATY SEITAN TACOS

SEITAN AND SAUSAGE CASSOULET

HEARTY STEW

STUFFED BELL PEPPERS

DRUNKEN "CHICKEN" WITH BROWN RICE

WHO NEEDS MEAT MEAT SAUCE

OLD-FASHIONED BEANS AND WEENIES

TOFU-FREE SLOPPY JOES

CHAPTER NINE

Meat Alternatives

Cruciferous Vegetables, Tofu, and Rice

MAKES 6 SERVINGS

Napa cabbage is another name for Chinese cabbage, which has been cultivated in East Asia for millennia and was first grown in the Napa, California, area in the United States. It is a Chinese vegetable that can stand up to longer cooking.

1 (16-OUNCE) PACKAGE FIRM TOFU, PREPARED
    TO COOK (PAGE 14), CUBED
2 CUPS CHOPPED BOK CHOY
2 CUPS CHOPPED NAPA CABBAGE
½ CUP CHOPPED WHITE ONION
½ CUP CHOPPED CELERY
½ CUP HALVED PEAPODS
SLOW-COOKED BROWN BASMATI RICE (PAGE 22)

1. Combine the tofu, bok choy, cabbage, onion, celery, and peapods in the slow cooker.

2. Cover and cook on low for 6 hours.

3. Serve hot with the rice.

Crispy Tofu and Brown Basmati Rice

MAKES 6 SERVINGS

Sweet-and-sour sauce gives this crispy tofu a tangy flavor. These contrasting flavors complement each other as well as the tofu and vegetables in this dish. The ingredients in sweet-and-sour sauces can vary; however, the primary ingredients usually include sugar, pineapple, bell peppers, distilled vinegar, and cornstarch.

1 (16-OUNCE) PACKAGE EXTRA-FIRM TOFU, PREPARED
    TO COOK (PAGE 14), CUBED

1 TABLESPOON CORNSTARCH

2 TABLESPOONS VEGETABLE OIL

1 CUP BROCCOLI FLORETS

1 CUP SLICED CARROTS

1 LARGE YELLOW BELL PEPPER, SEEDED AND CHOPPED

½ LARGE WHITE ONION, CHOPPED

1 (8-OUNCE) CAN SLICED WATER CHESTNUTS, RINSED AND DRAINED

1 (10-OUNCE) BOTTLE SWEET-AND-SOUR SAUCE

SLOW-COOKED BROWN BASMATI RICE (PAGE 22)

1. Combine the tofu and cornstarch in a gallon-size zip-top plastic bag, seal, and shake the bag to coat the tofu.

2. Heat the vegetable oil in a large skillet over medium heat until hot.

3. Add the tofu to the skillet and cook until the tofu has a crunchy coating, about 15 minutes on each side.

4. Transfer the tofu to the slow cooker.

5. Add the broccoli, carrots, bell pepper, onion, and water chestnuts to the slow cooker.

6. Pour the bottle of sweet-and-sour sauce over the top of the tofu and the vegetables and stir to mix well.

7. Cover and cook on low for 3 hours.

8. Serve hot with the rice.

Barbecue-Style Tofu and Pineapple

MAKES 6 SERVINGS

Tofu is a great resource for vegetarians and vegans alike. It has the ability to take on the flavors of other foods and provides great texture and substance. Tofu in barbecue sauce would fit in perfectly at a cookout; plug in your slow cooker outside and let your meat-eating guests enjoy the aromas from the pot. You might even share some with them. Serve hot over your favorite grain, or cooled off over salad greens.

NONSTICK COOKING SPRAY

1 LARGE YELLOW ONION, CHOPPED

8 LARGE GARLIC CLOVES, MINCED

1½ CUPS CANNED CRUSHED PINEAPPLE IN ITS OWN JUICE

½ CUP PITTED DATES

2 FRESH HOT CHILES, CHOPPED

1 (2-INCH) PIECE FRESH GINGER, PEELED AND MINCED

⅓ CUP WATER

⅓ CUP TOMATO PASTE

2 TABLESPOONS TAMARI

1 TABLESPOON FRESH LIME JUICE

1 TABLESPOON APPLE CIDER VINEGAR

CRACKED BLACK PEPPER, TO TASTE

2 (14-OUNCE) PACKAGES EXTRA-FIRM TOFU, PREPARED
    TO COOK (PAGE 14), CUBED

SEA SALT, TO TASTE

1. Lightly spray the slow cooker with the nonstick cooking spray.

2. In a nonstick skillet over medium heat, sauté the onion in a small amount of water.

3. Add the garlic to the skillet and cook for an additional minute.

4. Scrape the onion and the garlic into a blender or food processor.

5. Add the crushed pineapple and its juice, pitted dates, chiles, ginger, water, tomato paste, tamari, lime juice, apple cider vinegar, and black pepper to the blender or food processor.

6. Purée the ingredients on high until the sauce has a smooth, uniform consistency.

7. Place the tofu in the slow cooker.

8. Pour the sauce from the blender or food processor over the tofu.

9. Stir the sauce and the tofu very gently to ensure that all sides of the tofu are covered.

10. Cover and cook on low for 8 hours.

11. Add the sea salt.

12. Serve hot or cold.

Tofu Sloppy Joes

MAKES 6 SERVINGS

Sloppy joes are an American tradition. This classic sandwich is typically made with ground beef, onions, seasonings, and tomato sauce. The only difference between the original sloppy joe and Tofu Sloppy Joes is the tofu. Packed with protein and virtually no saturated fat, Tofu Sloppy Joes are sure to be the next great American tradition (at least among vegans).

1 SMALL YELLOW ONION, DICED

1 SMALL GREEN BELL PEPPER, SEEDED AND CHOPPED

½ TEASPOON GARLIC SALT

1 (16-OUNCE) PACKAGE EXTRA-FIRM TOFU, PREPARED
    TO COOK (PAGE 14), CUBED

1 TEASPOON DRIED OREGANO

1 TEASPOON DRIED BASIL

2 CUPS TOMATO SAUCE

WHOLE-GRAIN BUNS

1. In a small nonstick skillet, sauté the yellow onion, green pepper, and garlic salt in a small amount of water.

2. Add the tofu, oregano, basil, and tomato sauce to the onion mixture and stir.

3. Transfer the tofu mixture to the slow cooker.

4. Cover and cook on low for 6 to 8 hours.

5. Serve hot on the whole-grain buns.

Tofu and Spinach Lasagna

MAKES 4 TO 6 SERVINGS

Who doesn't love a good lasagna? And who doesn't hate the time and energy it takes to prepare regular lasagna in the oven? This vegan version eliminates all the kitchen hassles and spares your arteries in the process. Serve with a green salad with Italian dressing and warm crusty bread.

2 (16-OUNCE) PACKAGES FIRM TOFU, PREPARED TO COOK (PAGE 14)

¼ CUP SOY MILK

2 TABLESPOONS FRESH LEMON JUICE

1 TABLESPOON SUGAR

3 TEASPOONS MINCED FRESH BASIL

2 TEASPOONS SEA SALT

½ TEASPOON GARLIC POWDER

2 (10-OUNCE) PACKAGES FROZEN CHOPPED SPINACH, THAWED
    AND DRAINED

4 CUPS TOMATO SAUCE

8 OUNCES UNCOOKED LASAGNA NOODLES

GARLIC BREAD (OPTIONAL)

1. In a blender or food processor, purée the tofu, soy milk, lemon juice, sugar, fresh basil, sea salt, and garlic powder until the mixture reaches a smooth consistency.

2. Add the spinach to the blender or food processor and mix well.

3. Pour 1 cup of tomato sauce over the bottom of the slow cooker.

4. Start the layering process with one-third of the uncooked noodles, one-third of the tofu-spinach mixture, and 1 cup tomato sauce.

5. Repeat the layering process two more times, ending with the tomanto sauce.

7. Cover and cook on low for 6 to 8 hours, or until the noodles reach the desired tenderness.

8. Serve hot with the garlic bread.

Tempeh with Almond Butter

MAKES 8 SERVINGS

Mushrooms are a good source of vitamin B12 (riboflavin), a vitamin that is essential for everyone, not just vegans. The brown creminis used here have more flavor than white mushrooms. Over the course of the cooking process, this dish will appear to have too much liquid. Don't be concerned. The liquid will eventually dissipate and leave you with a thickened dish perfect for serving with Slow-Cooked Brown Basmati Rice (page 22).

4 CUPS VEGETABLE STOCK (PAGE 20)

2 (8-OUNCE) PACKAGES THREE-GRAIN TEMPEH, LIGHTLY STEAMED

1½ CUPS SHREDDED CARROTS

8 OUNCES CREMINI MUSHROOMS, SLICED

¾ CUP NATURAL ALMOND BUTTER

2 LARGE RED BELL PEPPERS, SEEDED AND CHOPPED

1 LARGE SWEET POTATO, PEELED AND CUBED

2 TABLESPOONS SOY SAUCE

2 TEASPOONS GROUND GINGER

1 TEASPOON CAYENNE PEPPER

1 TEASPOON SEASONED SALT

1 TEASPOON CRACKED BLACK PEPPER

1. Combine the vegetable stock, tempeh, carrots, mushrooms, almond butter, bell peppers, sweet potato, and soy sauce in the slow cooker.

2. Stir in the ginger, cayenne pepper, seasoned salt, and black pepper.

3. Cover and cook on low for 8 to 10 hours.

4. Serve hot.

Peanut, Tempeh, and Butternut Squash Mole

MAKES 6 SERVINGS

Mole might not be familiar to you. Mole (pronounced MOH-lay) is the name for a variety of sauces used in Mexican cuisine, usually featuring chiles, chocolate, nuts or seeds, and onions.

1 DRIED CHILE, SEEDED AND CUT INTO ½-INCH PIECES

1½ CUPS HOT VEGETABLE STOCK (PAGE 20)

1 MEDIUM WHITE ONION, CHOPPED

3 GARLIC CLOVES, MINCED

½ TEASPOON CHILI POWDER

½ TEASPOON GROUND CINNAMON

¼ TEASPOON GROUND ALLSPICE

⅛ TEASPOON GROUND CLOVES

⅛ TEASPOON CRACKED BLACK PEPPER

1 CUP CANNED DICED FIRE-ROASTED TOMATOES, DRAINED

⅓ CUP NATURAL PEANUT BUTTER

½ TEASPOON SEA SALT

1 SLICE WHOLE-WHEAT BREAD, TORN IN PIECES

½ TO 1 CANNED CHIPOTLE PEPPER IN ADOBO SAUCE

NONSTICK COOKING SPRAY

3 (8-OUNCE) PACKAGES TEMPEH, LIGHTLY STEAMED AND CUT INTO
    ¾-INCH CUBES

1 POUND BUTTERNUT SQUASH, PEELED AND CUT INTO ¾-INCH CUBES

1 TEASPOON SUGAR (OPTIONAL)

SLOW-COOKED BROWN BASMATI RICE (PAGE 22) (OPTIONAL)

TORTILLAS (OPTIONAL)

1. In a small bowl, cover the dried chile with ½ cup of the hot vegetable stock. Set aside to soften for about 30 minutes.

continued ▶

2. In a small nonstick skillet, sauté the onion in a small amount of water until it begins to brown, 5 to 10 minutes.

3. Add the garlic and cook for an additional minute.

4. Transfer the onion and garlic mixture to a blender or food processor.

5. Add the chili powder, cinnamon, allspice, cloves, black pepper, dried chile with its soaking liquid, tomatoes, and remaining 1 cup vegetable stock to a blender or food processor and blend or process for 10 seconds.

6. Add the natural peanut butter, sea salt, whole-wheat bread, and chipotle pepper.

7. Blend or process all the ingredients until the mixture is nearly smooth.

8. Lightly spray the slow cooker with the nonstick cooking spray.

9. Place the tempeh and squash in the bottom of the slow cooker.

10. Pour the contents of the blender or food processor over the tempeh and squash.

11. Stir the ingredients in the slow cooker to ensure that the sauce covers all the surfaces.

12. Cover and cook on low for 3 to 6 hours, or until the sauce is thick and the squash is tender.

13. Before serving, check the sauce and add the sugar, if desired.

14. Serve hot with the rice or as a filling for tortillas.

Tempeh Enchilada Casserole

MAKES 6 SERVINGS

Having a theme night for dinner once a week is a great way to keep mealtime lively and interesting. Mexican night is a favorite theme for many households, and with an enchilada casserole, a successful Mexican night is on the way. Serve hot with a dollop of vegan sour cream and a side of Mexican rice.

2 (15-OUNCE) CANS BLACK BEANS, RINSED AND DRAINED

1 (28-OUNCE) CAN DICED TOMATOES, UNDRAINED

1 (15-OUNCE) CAN CORN, DRAINED

1 (14-OUNCE) JAR CHUNKY SALSA

1 (6-OUNCE) CAN TOMATO PASTE

1 (8-OUNCE) PACKAGE TEMPEH, LIGHTLY STEAMED AND CRUMBLED

1 (4-OUNCE) CAN DICED GREEN CHILES, DRAINED

2 TEASPOONS GROUND CUMIN

2 TEASPOONS CHILI POWDER

2 GARLIC CLOVES, MINCED

6 CORN TORTILLAS

1 CUP SHREDDED VEGAN CHEDDAR CHEESE

1 (2-OUNCE) CAN SLICED BLACK OLIVES, DRAINED

1. In a large bowl, combine the black beans, diced tomatoes with their juices, corn, chunky salsa, tomato paste, tempeh, green chiles, ground cumin, chili powder, and garlic and mix well.

2. Spread 1 cup of the black bean mixture in the bottom of the slow cooker.

3. Top with 2 corn tortillas.

4. Sprinkle one-third of the shredded vegan cheddar cheese on top of the corn tortillas.

5. Repeat the layering (bean mixture, corn tortillas, vegan cheese) two more times, ending with cheese.

continued ▶

6. Sprinkle the black olives over the top.

7. Cover and cook on low for 3 to 3½ hours.

8. Serve hot.

Portobello Mushroom and Tempeh Stroganoff

MAKES 6 TO 8 SERVINGS

Stroganoff is a dish usually made with beef, noodles, mushrooms, and sour cream. Leave it to a vegan to turn the tables. As long as the main ingredients in the dish—in this case, mushrooms and tempeh—are cooked in a sauce containing sour cream, the dish can qualify as a stroganoff. Simply substitute soy sour cream for the real thing.

2 (8-OUNCE) PACKAGES TEMPEH, LIGHTLY STEAMED AND CRUMBLED

1 CUP SOY SOUR CREAM

1 CUP SOY MILK

1 (11-OUNCE) CONTAINER VEGAN MUSHROOM GRAVY

2 POUNDS PORTOBELLO MUSHROOMS, STEMS REMOVED, CAPS SLICED INTO 1-INCH PIECES

1 (16-OUNCE) PACKAGE FROZEN PEAS AND CARROTS

2 CELERY STALKS, SLICED

1 TABLESPOON DRIED THYME

2 TEASPOONS DRIED SAGE

2 BAY LEAVES

SEA SALT AND CRACKED BLACK PEPPER, TO TASTE

1 (16-OUNCE) PACKAGE EGG-FREE NOODLES, COOKED

1. Combine the tempeh, soy sour cream, soy milk, and vegan mushroom gravy in the slow cooker.

2. Stir in the mushrooms, peas and carrots, celery, thyme, sage, and bay leaves.

3. Season with the sea salt and black pepper.

4. Cover and cook on low for 6 to 8 hours.

5. Remove the bay leaves.

6. Serve hot over the egg-free noodles.

Tempeh and Tofu Hungarian Goulash

MAKES 6 SERVINGS

Goulash originated in Hungary and is still one of that nation's national dishes. A stew consisting of meat, vegetables, and noodles, goulash contains another important component: paprika. There's plenty of paprika here, but instead of meat, this dish includes both tempeh and tofu for a double dose of soy protein. Tempeh is a fermented soy product that originates in Indonesia. It can be found at health food stores and many grocery stores.

8 OUNCES TEMPEH, LIGHTLY STEAMED AND CUT INTO ¾-INCH PIECES

12 OUNCES WHITE MUSHROOMS, SLICED

1 CUP DICED CARROT

2 MEDIUM WHITE POTATOES, PEELED AND CUT INTO 1-INCH PIECES

1¼ CUPS VEGETABLE STOCK (PAGE 20)

2 MEDIUM YELLOW ONIONS, ROUGHLY CHOPPED

1 LARGE TOMATO, ROUGHLY CHOPPED

1 SMALL GREEN BELL PEPPER, SEEDED AND ROUGHLY CHOPPED

2 GARLIC CLOVES, SMASHED

2 TABLESPOONS PAPRIKA

1 TABLESPOON DRIED PARSLEY

2 TEASPOONS DRIED DILL

½ TEASPOON CARAWAY SEEDS, LIGHTLY CRUSHED

½ TEASPOON SEA SALT

¼ TEASPOON CRACKED BLACK PEPPER

1 (12-OUNCE) PACKAGE SILKEN TOFU

1 CUP FROZEN PEAS, THAWED

1 (12-OUNCE) PACKAGE ELBOW MACARONI, COOKED

1. Combine the tempeh, mushrooms, carrot, and potatoes in the slow cooker.

2. Combine the vegetable stock, onions, tomato, bell pepper, and garlic in a blender or food processor and purée.

3. Stir the puréed mixture into the slow cooker.

4. Add the paprika, parsley, dill, caraway seeds, sea salt and black pepper.

5. Cover and cook on low for 8 to 10 hours.

6. At the end of the cooking process take a small amount of liquid from the slow cooker and purée it with the silken tofu in a blender or food processor until very smooth.

7. Stir the tofu purée into the slow cooker.

8. Add the peas to the slow cooker and allow the peas to heat through.

9. Serve hot over the elbow macaroni.

Chunky Seitan Roast

MAKES 4 SERVINGS

Seitan is a popular food among Buddhists as well as in the macrobiotic diet. Seitan is also a great alternative to tofu and tempeh for those who are allergic to soy. Serve a green salad alongside this roast.

NONSTICK COOKING SPRAY

8 OUNCES SLOW-COOKED SEITAN (PAGE 24), CUT INTO CHUNKS

1 TABLESPOON OLIVE OIL

2 SMALL SWEET ONIONS, QUARTERED

1 POUND BABY CARROTS

1 POUND SMALL NEW POTATOES, SCRUBBED AND QUARTERED

SEA SALT AND CRACKED BLACK PEPPER, TO TASTE

1½ CUPS VEGETABLE STOCK (PAGE 20)

¼ CUP DRY RED WINE

2 GARLIC CLOVES, CRUSHED

½ TEASPOON DRIED THYME

1. Lightly spray the slow cooker with the nonstick cooking spray.

2. Place the seitan in the slow cooker.

3. In a large skillet, heat the olive oil over medium-high heat.

4. Add the onions, baby carrots, and new potatoes to the skillet and brown quickly.

5. Season with the sea salt and black pepper.

6. Transfer the seasoned vegetables to the slow cooker.

7. Add the vegetable stock, dry red wine, garlic, and thyme and stir well.

8. Cover and cook on low for 6 to 8 hours.

9. Arrange the seitan and vegetables on a serving platter and spoon the cooking liquid over the entire dish.

10. Serve hot.

Meaty Seitan Tacos

MAKES 4 TO 8 SERVINGS

Dress up these Meaty Seitan Tacos with shredded lettuce, diced tomatoes, guacamole, shredded vegan cheddar cheese, and black olives, and top with vegan sour cream. These tacos are great when you want something special for the kids or when you know people are dropping by.

16 OUNCES SLOW-COOKED SEITAN (PAGE 24), CRUMBLED

1 CUP VEGETABLE STOCK (PAGE 20)

⅔ CUP SALSA

½ CUP CHOPPED FRESH CILANTRO

1½ TEASPOONS MINCED GARLIC

1 TEASPOON MAPLE SYRUP

1 TEASPOON GROUND CUMIN

½ TEASPOON SEA SALT

JUICE OF 1 LIME

8 TACO SHELLS

1. In a large nonstick skillet, lightly brown the seitan over medium-high heat.

2. Transfer the seitan to the slow cooker.

3. Stir in the vegetable stock, salsa, cilantro, garlic, maple syrup, cumin, sea salt, and lime juice.

4. Cover and cook on low for 5 to 6 hours.

5. Serve hot in the taco shells.

Seitan and Sausage Cassoulet

MAKES 4 SERVINGS

The cassole *is a deep, round cooking vessel used in France to prepare cassou-let. Cassoulet is traditionally made with goose, duck, mutton, or pork sausage, and is accompanied by white beans. This vegan cassoulet breaks with French tradition and uses seitan and vegan sausage instead of meat. In France it is a complete meal.*

NONSTICK COOKING SPRAY

2 CUPS VEGETABLE STOCK (PAGE 20)

1 (15-OUNCE) CAN WHITE BEANS, RINSED AND DRAINED

1 (14½-OUNCE) CAN DICED TOMATOES, UNDRAINED

1½ CUPS SLOW-COOKED SEITAN (PAGE 24), CUBED

½ TUBE VEGAN SAUSAGE, BROWNED

3 SMALL CARROTS, CHOPPED

2 STALKS CELERY, CHOPPED

1 SMALL YELLOW ONION, MINCED

1 TABLESPOON HERBS DE PROVENCE

1 TEASPOON DRIED ROSEMARY

1 TEASPOON DRIED THYME

½ TEASPOON SMOKED PAPRIKA

2 BAY LEAVES

SEA SALT, TO TASTE

1. Lightly spray the slow cooker with the nonstick cooking spray.

2. Combine the vegetable stock, beans, tomatoes with their juices, seitan, vegan sausage, carrots, celery, and onion in the slow cooker.

3. Stir in the herbs de Provence, rosemary, thyme, paprika, bay leaves, and sea salt.

4. Cover and cook on low for 6 to 8 hours.

5. Remove the bay leaves.

6. Ladle the cassoulet into bowls and serve hot.

Hearty Stew

MAKES 4 SERVINGS

Potatoes, carrots, seitan, and cashew butter make this a hearty and healthful meal. The potatoes and carrots take care of your carbohydrates, the seitan your protein, and the cashew butter your fats. All your macronutrient needs are covered, and with some lightly toasted whole-grain bread, so is dinner.

8 OUNCES SLOW-COOKED SEITAN (PAGE 24), CUT INTO BITE-SIZE PIECES

4 MEDIUM POTATOES, PEELED AND CUT INTO BITE-SIZE PIECES

4 LARGE CARROTS, SLICED

1 LARGE LEEK, THINLY SLICED

3 GARLIC CLOVES, MINCED

1 (8-OUNCE) CAN TOMATO SAUCE

1 CUP VEGETABLE STOCK (PAGE 20)

¼ CUP NATURAL CASHEW BUTTER

2 TABLESPOONS SOY SAUCE

½ TEASPOON GROUND GINGER

1. Combine the seitan, potatoes, carrots, leek, and garlic in the slow cooker.

2. In a medium bowl, whisk together the tomato sauce, vegetable stock, cashew butter, soy sauce, and ginger.

3. Pour the tomato sauce mixture over the ingredients in the slow cooker.

4. Cover and cook on low for 10 to 12 hours.

5. Ladle the stew into bowls and serve hot.

Stuffed Bell Peppers

MAKES 6 SERVINGS

Stuffed peppers are traditionally made with ground beef; in this dish the ground beef has been replaced with veggie crumbles, which provide a new flavor and a vegan twist. Green bell peppers fit into a variety of diets, not only a vegan one. This vegetable can be part of an anti-inflammatory, low-glycemic, or diabetic diet. Green bell peppers provide 159 percent of the recommended daily intake of vitamin C. Serve these stuffed peppers with a green salad on the side.

1 POUND VEGGIE CRUMBLES

1 CUP COOKED BROWN RICE

1 (14½-OUNCE) CAN ITALIAN TOMATOES, DRAINED, LIQUID RESERVED

2 TABLESPOONS KETCHUP

1 TEASPOON VEGAN WORCESTERSHIRE SAUCE

1 TEASPOON CRACKED BLACK PEPPER

6 MEDIUM GREEN BELL PEPPERS, TOPS REMOVED AND RESERVED, SEEDED

⅓ CUP WATER

1. In a medium bowl, thoroughly combine the veggie crumbles and brown rice with the Italian tomatoes, ketchup, vegan Worcestershire sauce, and black pepper.

2. If more moisture is needed, slowly add the reserved liquid from the tomatoes until the desired consistency is reached.

3. Stuff each pepper with an equal amount of the veggie crumble and rice mixture.

4. Nestle the peppers in the slow cooker and put the pepper tops back on.

5. Pour the water around the bases of the peppers.

6. Cover and cook on low for 6 to 8 hours.

7. Serve hot.

Drunken "Chicken" with Brown Rice

No chicken was harmed or forced to drink alcohol in the making of this dish. The alcohol consumption is reserved for the recipients of this beautiful meal. The dry white wine brings the vegan chicken alive with flavor and the rice adds whole-grain substance to the dish. Enjoy with a glass of white wine to satisfy your palate even more.

2½ CUPS VEGETABLE STOCK (PAGE 20)

2 CUPS UNCOOKED CONVERTED LONG-GRAIN RICE

1½ CUPS DICED VEGAN CHICKEN

½ CUP CHOPPED WHITE ONION

⅓ CUP FROZEN PEAS

¼ CUP DRY WHITE WINE

2 CELERY STALKS, CHOPPED

1 LARGE CARROT, CHOPPED

CHOPPED FRESH PARSLEY, FOR GARNISH

1. Combine the vegetable stock, rice, vegan chicken, onion, peas, wine, celery, and carrot in the slow cooker and stir.

2. Cover and cook on low for 6 to 8 hours.

3. Stir well and serve hot, garnished with the fresh parsley.

Who Needs Meat Meat Sauce

MAKES 8 SERVINGS

And who needs a spaghetti pot? Here, the spaghetti cooks right in the slow cooker. Faux meat tastes so good that even your non-vegan friends won't know the difference. Serve this sauce at your next dinner party with a large green salad and some fresh garlic bread, and no one will be the wiser.

2 (28-OUNCE) CANS WHOLE PLUM TOMATOES, UNDRAINED

1 (12-OUNCE) PACKAGE VEGAN SOY CRUMBLES

1 LARGE GREEN BELL PEPPER, SEEDED AND FINELY CHOPPED

1 LARGE YELLOW ONION, CHOPPED

3 GARLIC CLOVES, MINCED

2 TABLESPOONS BALSAMIC VINEGAR

1 TEASPOON DRIED BASIL

½ TEASPOON SUGAR

½ TEASPOON SEA SALT

12 OUNCES UNCOOKED SPAGHETTI, BROKEN INTO THIRDS

1 CUP BOILING WATER

¼ CUP CHOPPED FRESH BASIL

2 TABLESPOONS CHOPPED FRESH PARSLEY

1. Combine the tomatoes with their juices, soy crumbles, bell pepper, onion, garlic, vinegar, basil, sugar, and sea salt in the slow cooker, breaking up the tomatoes with a wooden spoon.

2. Cover and cook on low for 5 hours or on high for 3½ hours.

3. Add the spaghetti, water, basil, and parsley.

4. Cover and cook for an additional hour, or until the pasta is tender.

5. Serve hot.

Old-Fashioned Beans and Weenies

MAKES 8 SERVINGS

Most of us grew up with beans and weenies, baked beans with little pieces of hot dogs thrown in. There's no reason that tradition can't continue with a version that doesn't contain all the fat, nitrates, and guilt. This vegan version is just as good if not better, and can accompany any good potato salad, coleslaw, or other favorite summer dish.

1 TABLESPOON VEGETABLE STOCK (PAGE 20)

1 CUP MOLASSES

1 CUP PACKED BROWN SUGAR

1 TEASPOON MUSTARD POWDER

1 TEASPOON VEGAN WORCESTERSHIRE SAUCE

½ TEASPOON SEA SALT

4 (15-OUNCE) CANS GREAT NORTHERN BEANS, RINSED AND DRAINED

½ CUP WATER

4 VEGAN HOT DOGS, SLICED

1 LARGE WHITE ONION, DICED

1. In a large bowl, combine the vegetable stock, molasses, brown sugar, dry mustard, vegan Worcestershire sauce, and sea salt and stir well.

2. Place one-third of the beans in the slow cooker and add a small amount of the water.

3. Layer one-third of the brown sugar mixture, one-third of the vegan hot dogs, and one-third of the onion on top of the beans in the slow cooker.

4. Repeat the layering process two more times, adding a small amount of the water with each layer.

5. Cover and cook on low heat for 6 to 8 hours.

6. Serve warm or cold.

Tofu-Free Sloppy Joes

MAKES 4 TO 5 SERVINGS

If you're allergic to soy or just don't care for it, these lentil sloppy joes are just as good, just as nutritious, and just as fun. When you're looking for food a little closer to its natural state, lentils are a great alternative to meat substitutes.

1 (14½-OUNCE) CAN DICED TOMATOES, UNDRAINED

1½ CUPS VEGETABLE STOCK (PAGE 20)

1 CUP DRIED GREEN LENTILS, RINSED

¾ CUP CHOPPED YELLOW ONION

5 TABLESPOONS TOMATO PASTE

½ LARGE RED BELL PEPPER, SEEDED AND CHOPPED

1 TABLESPOON MINCED GARLIC

1 TABLESPOON APPLE CIDER VINEGAR

2 TEASPOONS DRIED PARSLEY

1 TABLESPOON CHILI POWDER

1½ TEASPOONS DRIED OREGANO

1½ TEASPOONS SMOKED PAPRIKA

1 TEASPOON SEA SALT

¼ TEASPOON CAYENNE PEPPER

CRACKED BLACK PEPPER, TO TASTE

WHOLE-GRAIN BUNS

1. Combine the tomatoes with their juices, vegetable stock, lentils, onion, tomato paste, bell pepper, garlic, and vinegar in the slow cooker.

2. Stir in the parsley, chili powder, oregano, paprika, sea salt, cayenne pepper, and black pepper.

3. Cover and cook on low for 7 to 8 hours or on high for 3 to 4 hours, or until the lentils are tender.

4. If too much liquid remains in the slow cooker, remove the cover and cook on high for an additional 30 to 60 minutes.

5. Serve hot on whole-grain buns.

International Cuisine

ASIAN POTATO SALAD

VIETNAMESE NOODLE SOUP

CHINESE HOT POT

ASIAN FALL VEGETABLE STEW

"CHICKEN" CHOW MEIN

MEXICAN-STYLE MINESTRONE

MEXICAN RICE WITH BLACK
   BEANS AND SALSA

ENCHILADA WRAPS

BLACK BEAN TACOS

MEXICAN-STYLE LASAGNA

SWEETENED FRUIT CURRY

SWEET POTATO AND APPLE CURRY

CHICKPEA COCONUT CURRY

KIDNEY BEAN CURRY
   AND BASMATI RICE

CURRIED RICE AND LENTILS

International Cuisine

Asian Potato Salad

MAKES 8 TO 10 SERVINGS

Hot potato salad is much more common than you might think, so why not make it in the slow cooker? This Asian-inspired salad will be as big a hit as any cold potato salad at your next backyard get-together. The mandarin oranges seal the deal.

1 POUND FRESH BEAN SPROUTS

1 (6-OUNCE) CAN SLICED WATER CHESTNUTS, DRAINED

6 TO 8 RED POTATOES, CUBED

3 CELERY STALKS, SLICED

WATER, AS NEEDED

3 TABLESPOONS SESAME SEEDS

1 TEASPOON TOASTED SESAME OIL

8 TO 10 ROMAINE LETTUCE LEAVES, TORN

SOY SAUCE (OPTIONAL)

1 (8-OUNCE) CAN MANDARIN ORANGES, DRAINED (OPTIONAL)

1 CUP CRISPY CHINESE NOODLES (OPTIONAL)

1. Combine the bean sprouts, water chestnuts, potatoes, and celery in the slow cooker and add just enough water to cover.

2. Cover and cook on low for 6 to 8 hours.

3. Drain the liquid from the slow cooker.

4. Add the sesame seeds and the sesame oil to the slow cooker and stir well to coat the potatoes.

5. Arrange the potatoes on a bed of lettuce.

6. Serve hot with the soy sauce, mandarin oranges, and Chinese noodles, if desired.

Vietnamese Noodle Soup

MAKES 8 SERVINGS

The star anise used here imparts a strong taste of licorice. It can be found in Asian specialty stores and some supermarkets. This spice is easily recognizable by its star shape. Star anise can be ground but is typically used whole, as in this soup. Like a bay leaf, star anise should be removed before serving. Straining the stock removes the star anise while still preserving its flavor in the dish.

12 CUPS VEGETABLE STOCK (PAGE 20)

6 TABLESPOONS SOY SAUCE

6 SLICES FRESH GINGER

2 MEDIUM WHITE ONIONS, CHOPPED

2 RED CHILES, SEEDED AND CHOPPED

1 LARGE CARROT, DICED

2 WHOLE STAR ANISE

1 TEASPOON GROUND CINNAMON

¼ CUP WHITE MISO PASTE DISSOLVED IN ¼ CUPS HOT WATER

6 TABLESPOONS HOISIN SAUCE

3 TABLESPOONS FRESH LIME JUICE

12 OUNCES RICE NOODLES, SOAKED FOR 15 MINUTES IN
    COLD WATER AND DRAINED

BEAN SPROUTS (OPTIONAL)

CHOPPED SCALLIONS (OPTIONAL)

1. Pour the vegetable stock into the slow cooker.

2. Stir in the soy sauce, ginger, onions, chiles, carrot, star anise, and cinnamon.

3. Cover and cook on low for 6 hours.

4. Strain the contents of the slow cooker through a sieve and discard the solids.

5. Return the strained liquid to the slow cooker.

6. In a small bowl, combine the miso mixture, hoisin sauce, and lime juice and mix well.

7. Add the mixture to the slow cooker.

8. Stir in the rice noodles.

9. Cook for an additional 5 to 10 minutes, or until the rice noodles are soft.

10. Ladle the hot soup into bowls and top with the bean sprouts and chopped scallions, if desired.

Chinese Hot Pot

MAKES 4 SERVINGS

A hot pot is a vessel full of simmering stock that sits on the dinner table. Diners cook meats, seafood, and vegetables in the stock right at the table. The Chinese hot pot originated in Mongolia centuries ago. In Mongolia the hot pot is used to cook different types of meat, including horse and mutton, but this Chinese hot pot contains neither. The slow cooker can create a vegan stew that tastes like a hot pot meal but is much less trouble for guests.

1 (6-OUNCE) CAN SLICED WATER CHESTNUTS, DRAINED

1 LARGE CARROT, HALVED LENGTHWISE AND THINLY SLICED

1 SMALL YELLOW ONION, CHOPPED

1 CELERY STALK, THINLY SLICED

2 GARLIC CLOVES, FINELY MINCED

1 TEASPOON GRATED FRESH GINGER

¼ TEASPOON RED PEPPER FLAKES

5½ CUPS VEGETABLE STOCK (PAGE 20)

1 TABLESPOON TAMARI

8 OUNCES EXTRA-FIRM TOFU, DRAINED, PRESSED, AND DICED

4 OUNCES SHIITAKE MUSHROOMS, STEMMED AND THINLY SLICED

1 OUNCE SNOW PEAS, CUT INTO 1-INCH PIECES

3 SCALLIONS, CHOPPED

½ TEASPOON TOASTED SESAME OIL

SLOW-COOKED BROWN BASMATI RICE (PAGE 22)

1. Combine the water chestnuts, carrot, onion, celery, garlic, ginger, and red pepper flakes in the slow cooker.

2. Pour in the vegetable stock and tamari and stir.

3. Cover and cook on low for 8 hours.

4. About 20 minutes before serving, add the tofu, mushrooms, snow peas, and scallions to the slow cooker.

5. Drizzle the sesame oil over the vegetables.

6. Cover and cook until the mushrooms and snow peas are tender.

7. Serve immediately with the rice.

Asian Fall Vegetable Stew

MAKES 6 TO 8 SERVINGS

Sambal oelek, a chile-based sauce from Indonesia, is used here to spice up a vegetable stew. Depending on what type of sambal oelek you use, the heat can vary. Check the heat level of your sauce or the stew may be too spicy.

4 LARGE SWEET POTATOES, PEELED AND CUT INTO 2-INCH CHUNKS
1 LARGE BUTTERNUT SQUASH, PEELED, QUARTERED, AND CUT INTO
   2-INCH CHUNKS
10 OUNCES SHIITAKE MUSHROOMS, STEMMED AND HALVED
1 BUNCH SCALLIONS, CUT INTO 1-INCH PIECES
2 (14-OUNCE) CANS UNSWEETENED COCONUT MILK
1½ CUPS WATER
3 TABLESPOONS SOY SAUCE
2 TEASPOONS SAMBAL OELEK
1 TEASPOON SEA SALT
CHOPPED FRESH CILANTRO, FOR GARNISH
CHOPPED SALTED PEANUTS, FOR GARNISH

1. Combine the sweet potatoes, squash, mushrooms, and scallions in the slow cooker.

2. In a medium bowl, whisk together the coconut milk, water, soy sauce, sambal oelek, and sea salt.

3. Add the mixture to the slow cooker and stir.

4. Cover and cook on high for 4 hours, or until the vegetables are tender.

5. Ladle the stew into bowls, garnish with the fresh cilantro and peanuts, and serve hot.

"Chicken" Chow Mein

MAKES 4 TO 6 SERVINGS

Chow Mein is an Americanized version of a Chinese fried noodle dish. This vegan version of Chicken Chow Mein is an adaptation of what you would find at your favorite Chinese restaurant.

1 POUND VEGAN CHICKEN, CHOPPED

1 (14-OUNCE) CAN BEAN SPROUTS, DRAINED

1½ CUPS CHOPPED CELERY

1½ CUPS CHOPPED CARROTS

1 CUP VEGETABLE STOCK (PAGE 20)

1 (8-OUNCE) CAN SLICED WATER CHESTNUTS, DRAINED

6 SCALLIONS, CHOPPED

⅓ CUP SOY SAUCE

½ TEASPOON GROUND GINGER

¼ TEASPOON RED PEPPER FLAKES

¼ CUP CORNSTARCH DISSOLVED IN ⅓ CUP WATER

SLOW-COOKED BROWN BASMATI RICE (PAGE 22)

1. Combine the vegan chicken, bean sprouts, celery, and carrots in the slow cooker.

2. Pour in the vegetable stock.

3. Stir in the water chestnuts, scallions, soy sauce, ginger, and pepper flakes.

4. Cover and cook on low for 6 to 8 hours.

5. Stir the cornstarch mixture into the slow cooker.

6. Leave the lid askew to allow steam to escape and cook for an additional 30 minutes, or until thickened.

7. Serve hot with the rice.

Mexican-Style Minestrone

MAKES 6 SERVINGS

Minestrone, which originates from Italy, is a thick soup containing an assortment of vegetables and sometimes rice or pasta. A good minestrone can appeal to any type of palate, and there is no strict definition of what constitutes real minestrone. This Mexican-Style Minestrone is based on beans.

3 CUPS VEGETABLE STOCK (PAGE 20)

2 (15-OUNCE) CANS BLACK BEANS, RINSED AND DRAINED

1 (15-OUNCE) CAN CHICKPEAS, RINSED AND DRAINED

2 (14½-OUNCE) CANS STEWED TOMATOES

1 (15-OUNCE) CAN CORN, DRAINED

2 CUPS DICED RED POTATOES

2 CUPS FROZEN GREEN BEANS

1 CUP SALSA

1 TABLESPOON CHILI POWDER

SEA SALT AND CRACKED BLACK PEPPER, TO TASTE

CORNBREAD (OPTIONAL)

1. Combine the vegetable stock, black beans, chickpeas, stewed tomatoes, corn, potatoes, green beans, and salsa in the slow cooker.

2. Stir in the chili powder, sea salt, and black pepper.

3. Cover and cook on low for 8 to 9 hours or on high for 4 to 5 hours.

4. Serve hot with the cornbread, if desired.

Mexican Rice with Black Beans and Salsa

MAKES 6 SERVINGS

What would this Mexican rice with black beans be without salsa? It would still be really good, but fresh homemade salsa makes it even better. The foundation of this salsa, avocado, really works with the poblano chile (a mild to medium-hot chile) to provide a little kick (but not too much).

FOR THE RICE:

2 CUPS VEGETABLE STOCK (PAGE 20)

1 CUP UNCOOKED CONVERTED LONG-GRAIN RICE

1 CUP FINELY CHOPPED YELLOW ONION

2 (15-OUNCE) CANS BLACK BEANS, RINSED AND DRAINED

1 (4-OUNCE) CAN DICED GREEN CHILES, UNDRAINED

1 SMALL RED BELL PEPPER, SEEDED AND CHOPPED

1 SMALL GREEN BELL PEPPER, SEEDED AND CHOPPED

SEA SALT, TO TASTE

FOR THE SALSA:

1 LARGE AVOCADO, PEELED, PITTED, AND CUT INTO 1-INCH CUBES

3 TABLESPOONS FRESH LIME JUICE

1 LARGE FRESH POBLANO CHILE, MINCED

½ CUP DICED TOMATO

½ CUP THINLY SLICED SCALLIONS

½ CUP FINELY CHOPPED FRESH CILANTRO

2 TABLESPOONS OLIVE OIL

½ TEASPOON GROUND CUMIN

SEA SALT, TO TASTE

continued ▶

Make the rice:

1. Combine the vegetable stock, rice, and onion in the slow cooker and stir well.

2. Cover and cook on high for 1½ hours, or until the rice starts to become tender.

3. Stir the beans, chiles with their juices, red and green bell peppers, and sea salt into the slow cooker.

4. Cook on high for an additional 30 minutes, or until the rice is tender and the peppers are al dente.

Make the salsa:

1. In a large bowl, gently combine the avocado and the lime juice.

2. Add the poblano chile, tomato, scallions, cilantro, olive oil, cumin, and sea salt.

3. Gently combine all the ingredients.

4. Serve the beans and rice hot or warm with the salsa on top.

Enchilada Wraps

MAKES 6 TO 8 SERVINGS

Enchiladas, which originated in Mexico, are corn or flour tortillas wrapped around a filling of some sort and topped off with a chili sauce. These enchilada wraps meet the criteria and, served with a side of Mexican corn, make a complete meal.

1 (15-OUNCE) CAN KIDNEY BEANS, RINSED AND DRAINED

1 (15-OUNCE) CAN VEGAN REFRIED BEANS

1 CUP WATER

¾ CUP UNCOOKED CONVERTED LONG-GRAIN RICE

1 (4½-OUNCE) CAN DICED GREEN CHILES, DRAINED

½ CUP VEGAN SOUR CREAM

3 TABLESPOONS CHILI POWDER

6 TO 8 (6-INCH) FLOUR TORTILLAS

1 CUP SHREDDED VEGAN CHEDDAR CHEESE

1 (10-OUNCE) CAN ENCHILADA SAUCE

1. Combine the kidney beans, refried beans, water, rice, chiles, vegan sour cream, and chili powder in the slow cooker and stir well.

2. Cover and cook on low for 6 to 8 hours.

3. Place ½ cup of the bean mixture in the center of each tortilla.

4. Sprinkle the vegan shredded cheese on top of the bean mixture.

5. Wrap the tortilla around the filling.

6. Pour the enchilada sauce over the tortilla.

7. Serve hot.

Black Bean Tacos

MAKES 6 TO 12 SERVINGS

A two-part approach to these black bean tacos results in not only an appetizing and satisfying meal, but an aesthetically appealing one, too. The shells and toppings provide color and texture. Finish the tacos with black olives and vegan sour cream.

1 (15-OUNCE) CAN BLACK BEANS, RINSED AND DRAINED

1 (14½-OUNCE) CAN DICED TOMATOES, UNDRAINED

1 CUP UNCOOKED CONVERTED LONG-GRAIN RICE

1 CUP FROZEN CORN

2 GARLIC CLOVES, MINCED

1 TEASPOON CHILI POWDER

1 TEASPOON GROUND CUMIN

1 TEASPOON ONION POWDER

½ TEASPOON DRIED OREGANO

½ TEASPOON CAYENNE PEPPER

½ TEASPOON CELERY SALT

¼ TEASPOON CHIPOTLE PEPPER POWDER

12 TACO SHELLS

2 CUPS SHREDDED LETTUCE

8 OUNCES SHREDDED VEGAN CHEDDAR CHEESE

1 CUP SALSA

1. Combine the beans, tomatoes with their juices, rice, and corn in the slow cooker.

2. Stir in the garlic, chili powder, cumin, onion powder, oregano, cayenne pepper, celery salt, chipotle pepper powder.

3. Cover and cook on low for 5 hours.

4. Fill the taco shells with the taco filling and dress with the shredded lettuce, shredded vegan cheddar cheese, and salsa.

Mexican-Style Lasagna

MAKES 6 TO 8 SERVINGS

Is it Mexican night or Italian night? This lasagna can be served for either theme night and no one will argue, not because it's Italian (which it isn't), and not because it's Mexican (which it is), but because it's so good.

NONSTICK COOKING SPRAY

12 TO 14 SMALL CORN TORTILLAS

1 (28-OUNCE) CAN DICED TOMATOES, DRAINED

1 SMALL YELLOW ONION, CHOPPED

1 (15-OUNCE) CAN BLACK BEANS, RINSED AND DRAINED

2 CUPS SALSA

1 TABLESPOON FAJITA SEASONING

2 CUPS VEGAN CHICKEN

1 (15-OUNCE) CAN CORN, DRAINED

1 CUP SHREDDED VEGAN CHEDDAR CHEESE,

1 CUP SHREDDED VEGAN MOZZARELLA CHEESE

VEGAN SOUR CREAM (OPTIONAL)

1. Lightly spray the slow cooker with the nonstick cooking spray.

2. Arrange a single layer of tortillas in the bottom of the slow cooker.

3. Spread a layer of tomatoes across the tortillas.

4. Scatter some onions on top of the tomatoes.

5. Spread a layer of black beans on top of the onions.

6. Spread a layer of salsa over the black beans.

7. Sprinkle a generous amount of fajita seasoning over the salsa.

8. Spread a layer of vegan chicken over the seasoning.

9. Cover the vegan chicken with a layer of corn.

continued ▶

10. Top the corn with a layer of shredded vegan cheddar and shredded vegan mozzarella cheese.

11. Repeat the layers until the slow cooker is a little more than three-quarters full.

12. For the final layer, top the tortillas with the remaining tomatoes and vegan cheeses.

13. Cover and cook on low for 3 to 4 hours or on high for 2 hours.

14. Serve hot, topped with the vegan sour cream, if desired.

Sweetened Fruit Curry

MAKES 8 TO 10 SERVINGS

Curry dishes are often served with rice or some other accompaniment, but there is no need with this curry. Sweetened fruit curry can easily stand alone as breakfast, lunch, an appetizer, or even dessert. The varieties of fruit offered here are satisfying and bring a good dose of antioxidants and nutrients to this meal. If you do desire something a little extra, Arborio Rice (page 23) is a worthy addition.

1 (15-OUNCE) CAN UNSWEETENED PINEAPPLE CHUNKS, DRAINED

1 (15-OUNCE) CAN TROPICAL FRUIT COCKTAIL, DRAINED

1 (15-OUNCE) CAN SLICED YELLOW CLING PEACHES, DRAINED

½ (15-OUNCE) CAN APRICOT HALVES, DRAINED

7 TABLESPOONS VEGAN MARGARINE, MELTED

¼ CUP PACKED LIGHT BROWN SUGAR

1 TEASPOON CURRY POWDER

1½ TEASPOONS CORNSTARCH DISSOLVED IN 1½ TEASPOONS COLD WATER

1. Combine the pineapple, fruit cocktail, peaches, and apricots in the slow cooker.

2. In a medium bowl, thoroughly combine the vegan margarine, brown sugar, and curry powder.

3. Pour the vegan margarine mixture over the fruit in the slow cooker and stir gently.

4. Cover and cook on high for 2½ hours.

5. Stir the cornstarch mixture into the slow cooker.

6. Cook, uncovered, for an additional 30 minutes, or until the fruit is slightly thickened.

7. Serve hot or cold.

Sweet Potato and Apple Curry

MAKES 4 TO 6 SERVINGS

Spicy and sweet describes this curry perfectly. Sweet potatoes and apple bring the sweet, and the cabbage and seasonings bring the spice. When served over Slow-Cooked Brown Basmati Rice (page 22), this curry dish finds perfect balance.

2 TABLESPOONS OLIVE OIL

1 SMALL WHITE ONION, CHOPPED

1 TABLESPOON CURRY POWDER

½ TEASPOON GROUND CINNAMON

½ TEASPOON GARLIC POWDER

¼ TEASPOON CAYENNE PEPPER

¼ TEASPOON GROUND GINGER

2½ CUPS VEGETABLE STOCK (PAGE 20)

¾ CUP COOKED OR CANNED CHICKPEAS, RINSED AND DRAINED

½ CUP CHOPPED CARROTS

4 CELERY STALKS, CHOPPED

1 LARGE SWEET POTATO, PEELED AND DICED

1 LARGE APPLE, PEELED, CORED, AND CHOPPED

⅓ HEAD CABBAGE, SHREDDED

1 CUP LIGHT COCONUT MILK

SEA SALT AND CRACKED BLACK PEPPER, TO TASTE

1. Coat the bottom of the slow cooker with the olive oil.

2. Add the onion, curry powder, cinnamon, garlic powder, cayenne pepper, and ginger to the slow cooker and stir to coat the spices with the oil.

3. Add the vegetable stock, chickpeas, carrots, celery, sweet potato, apple, and cabbage and stir again.

4. Cover and cook on low for 6 hours, or until the sweet potatoes are thoroughly cooked.

5. At the end of the cooking process, stir in the coconut milk, sea salt, and black pepper.

6. Cook for an additional 15 minutes.

7. Serve hot.

Chickpea Coconut Curry

MAKES 4 TO 6 SERVINGS

Curry is a dish from India and Southeast Asia made up of a spice blend and meat or vegetables. Adding coconut creates a creamier curry while still embracing the spice. When chickpeas are thrown into the mix, the result is a high-protein meal with a distinctive ethnic flavor.

1 (15-OUNCE) CAN CHICKPEAS, RINSED AND DRAINED

3 CUPS CHOPPED CAULIFLOWER FLORETS

1 CUP FROZEN CUT GREEN BEANS

1 CUP SLICED CARROTS

½ CUP CHOPPED YELLOW ONION

1¾ CUPS VEGETABLE STOCK (PAGE 20)

1 TABLESPOON CURRY POWDER

1 (14-OUNCE) CAN LIGHT COCONUT MILK

¼ CUP SHREDDED FRESH BASIL

SLOW-COOKED BROWN BASMATI RICE (PAGE 22) (OPTIONAL)

1. Combine the chickpeas, cauliflower, green beans, carrots, and onion in the slow cooker.

2. Stir in the vegetable stock and curry powder.

3. Cover and cook on low for 5 to 6 hours or on high for 2½ to 3 hours.

4. Stir in the coconut milk and basil.

5. Ladle the curry over the rice and serve hot.

Kidney Bean Curry and Basmati Rice

MAKES 6 TO 8 SERVINGS

Kidney bean curry is known as rajma *in India. This slow-cooked kidney bean curry would actually be called* rajma chawal, *or* rajma *served with rice. How about some roti with your* rajma chawal? *Roti, an Indian bread made out of stone-ground whole-meal flour, is often served with curry and rice.*

2 (15-OUNCE) CANS KIDNEY BEANS, RINSED AND DRAINED

2 (14½-OUNCE) CANS DICED TOMATOES WITH CHILES, UNDRAINED

4 SMALL WHITE POTATOES, DICED

2 MEDIUM WHITE ONIONS, CHOPPED

1 TABLESPOON CURRY POWDER

1 TEASPOON CAYENNE PEPPER

½ TEASPOON GROUND CARDAMOM

½ TEASPOON GROUND GINGER

SLOW-COOKED BROWN BASMATI RICE (PAGE 22)

1. Combine the beans, tomatoes with their juices, potatoes, and onions in the slow cooker.

2. Stir in the curry powder, cayenne pepper, cardamom, and ginger.

3. Cover and cook on low for 6 to 9 hours or on high for 3 to 5 hours.

4. Ladle the curry over the rice and serve hot.

Curried Rice and Lentils

MAKES 4 SERVINGS

The curry powder used in this and many other curry dishes is often thought to originate from Indian cuisine. While garam masala, an authentic Indian spice blend, has some similarities to curry powder, this specific mixture of spices is actually a Western concoction.

3½ CUPS VEGETABLE STOCK (PAGE 20)

½ CUP DRIED LENTILS, RINSED

1 CUP UNCOOKED CONVERTED LONG-GRAIN RICE

1 SMALL WHITE ONION, DICED

2 TO 3 TEASPOONS CURRY POWDER

½ TEASPOON GARLIC POWDER

¼ TEASPOON CRACKED BLACK PEPPER

TABASCO SAUCE (OPTIONAL)

1. Pour the vegetable stock into the slow cooker.

2. Stir in the lentils, rice, onion, curry powder, garlic powder, and black pepper.

3. Cover and cook on low for 4 to 5 hours.

4. Serve hot with the Tabasco sauce, if desired.

CHAPTER ELEVEN

Desserts

BUTTERSCOTCH SAUCE

RICE PUDDING

SLOW-BAKED APPLES

CLASSIC APPLE COBBLER

PUMPKIN PIE

FUDGY BROWNIES

CHERRY PIE DROP CAKE

PEAR AND CHOCOLATE CAKE

CHOCOLATE-PEANUT BUTTER CAKE

NONTRADITIONAL BROWN BETTY

Desserts

Butterscotch Sauce

This recipe comes in handy when you need a dessert sauce with real substance, sweetness, and flavor. Serve at any temperature you like as a topping for non-dairy ice creams, cake, or any other dessert. To add an extra kick, add 2 tablespoons of your favorite Scotch, bourbon, or rum.

2½ CUPS VANILLA SOY CREAMER OR COCONUT CREAMER

1½ CUPS PACKED LIGHT BROWN SUGAR

¾ CUP BROWN RICE SYRUP

½ CUP VEGAN MARGARINE, MELTED

1 TABLESPOON VANILLA EXTRACT

PINCH OF SEA SALT

2 TABLESPOONS CORNSTARCH DISSOLVED IN 2 TABLESPOONS WATER

1. In a small slow cooker, whisk together the creamer, light brown sugar, brown rice syrup, vegan margarine, vanilla extract, and sea salt.

2. Cover and cook on low for 3 to 4 hours or on high for 1½ to 2 hours, or until the sauce is hot and bubbling around the edges.

3. In a small bowl, combine the cornstarch and the water and stir.

4. Add the cornstarch mixture to the slow cooker and stir.

5. Cook for an additional 5 to 10 minutes, or until the sauce thickens slightly.

6. Store the butterscotch sauce in the refrigerator in an airtight container for 7 to 10 days.

Rice Pudding

Rice pudding can be served as breakfast, dinner, or dessert. Historically, rice pudding is credited with being the Buddha's last meal before he entered an enlightened state. This pudding may not contribute quite that much to your life; however, it is tasty, filling, and, when prepared with dried fruit, quite nutritious.

4 CUPS VANILLA SOY MILK

1 CUP UNCOOKED ARBORIO RICE

1 CUP SUGAR

3 TABLESPOONS COLD VEGAN MARGARINE

1 TEASPOON VANILLA EXTRACT

½ TEASPOON GROUND CINNAMON

PINCH OF SEA SALT

¼ CUP CHOPPED DRIED CRANBERRIES OR CHERRIES (OPTIONAL)

¼ CUP CHOPPED DRIED APRICOTS (OPTIONAL)

1. Combine the soy milk, Arborio rice, sugar, vegan margarine, vanilla, cinnamon, and sea salt in the slow cooker and stir well.

2. Cover and cook on low for 2 to 4 hours, stirring often, until the pudding reaches the desired consistency.

3. Serve hot or cold, topped with the dried fruit, if desired.

Slow-Baked Apples

MAKES 4 SERVINGS

Apples are one of the healthiest foods in the world. They offer superior nutritional benefits and can be cooked in a variety of ways. Apples contain phytonutrients, including polyphenols, which can assist in weight loss by helping regulate blood sugar, an important component of any weight-loss plan.

NONSTICK COOKING SPRAY

4 LARGE BAKING APPLES, CORED

1 TABLESPOON FRESH LEMON JUICE

¾ CUP PACKED LIGHT BROWN SUGAR

½ CUP CHOPPED PECANS

⅓ CUP DRIED CRANBERRIES

¼ CUP VEGAN MARGARINE, SOFTENED

½ TEASPOON GROUND CINNAMON

½ CUP WATER

VANILLA SOY ICE CREAM (OPTIONAL)

1. Lightly spray the slow cooker with the nonstick cooking spray.

2. Peel the top of each apple down about 1 inch and brush the lemon juice on the cut surfaces.

3. In a medium bowl, combine the brown sugar, pecans, dried cranberries, vegan margarine, and cinnamon.

4. Spoon the mixture into the apple cavities.

5. Pour the water into the slow cooker and arrange the apples inside.

6. Cover and cook on low for 1 to 3 hours, or until the apples are tender.

7. Serve warm or at room temperature with the vanilla soy ice cream, if desired.

Classic Apple Cobbler

MAKES 4 TO 6 SERVINGS

Apples are enticing on their own, but what about making a classic fruit cobbler? Top with your favorite soy or coconut ice cream and you'll have a fabulous dessert.

4½ CUPS TART APPLES, PEELED, CORED, AND SLICED

⅓ CUP GRANULATED SUGAR

2 TABLESPOONS ALL-PURPOSE FLOUR

⅔ CUP ROLLED OATS

⅓ CUP DRIED CRANBERRIES

¼ TEASPOON GROUND CINNAMON

1 CUP WATER

3 TABLESPOONS VEGAN MARGARINE, MELTED

¾ CUP PACKED LIGHT BROWN SUGAR

VANILLA SOY ICE CREAM (OPTIONAL)

1. In a large bowl combine the apples, granulated sugar, and flour.

2. Mix in the oats, dried cranberries, and cinnamon.

3. Pour the water into the slow cooker.

4. Place the apple mixture in the water.

5. Drizzle the vegan margarine equally over the mixture.

6. Sprinkle with the brown sugar.

7. Cover and cook on low for 4 to 6 hours, or until the apples are tender.

8. Serve warm or at room temperature with the vanilla soy ice cream, if desired.

Pumpkin Pie

MAKES 8 SERVINGS

Limiting pumpkin pie to the fall and winter holidays deprives you of pumpkin's nutrient value. The canned pumpkin used in this Pumpkin Pie contains 540 percent of the recommended daily intake of vitamin A, compared to fresh pumpkin at only 26 percent. Pumpkin is also a very good source of dietary fiber, vitamin C, riboflavin, potassium, copper, and manganese. Pumpkin can play a protective role against heart disease and some forms of cancer when consumed on a regular basis.

NONSTICK COOKING SPRAY
1 (15-OUNCE) CAN PUMPKIN PURÉE
1⅓ CUPS NONDAIRY CREAMER
½ CUP PRE-MIXED BAKING PRODUCT
½ CUP GRANULATED SUGAR
¼ CUP PACKED LIGHT BROWN SUGAR
EGG SUBSTITUTE EQUIVALENT TO 2 EGGS
2 TABLESPOONS VEGAN MARGARINE, MELTED
2 TEASPOONS VANILLA EXTRACT
2½ TEASPOONS PUMPKIN PIE SPICE
NONDAIRY WHIPPED TOPPING (OPTIONAL)

1. Lightly spray the slow cooker with the nonstick cooking spray.

2. Combine the pumpkin, nondairy creamer, baking product, both sugars, egg substitute, vegan margarine, vanilla, and pumpkin pie spice in the slow cooker and mix well.

3. Cover and cook on low for 7 to 8 hours.

4. Serve hot or cold with the nondairy whipped topping, if desired.

Fudgy Brownies

MAKES 4 SERVINGS

The biggest hindrance to becoming vegan is the belief some people have that they can't live without foods like baked goods, which require dairy and eggs. These brownies provide the best of both worlds: a vegan slow-cooked goody that is just as fudgy, moist, and irresistible as any other brownie.

1¾ CUP PACKED LIGHT BROWN SUGAR

3 TABLESPOONS PLUS ¼ CUP UNSWEETENED COCOA POWDER

1 CUP ALL-PURPOSE FLOUR

½ CUP UNSWEETENED SOY MILK

2 TABLESPOONS OLIVE OIL

2 TEASPOONS BAKING POWDER

½ TEASPOON SEA SALT

½ TEASPOON VANILLA EXTRACT

1¾ CUP BOILING WATER

VANILLA SOY ICE CREAM (OPTIONAL)

1. In a large bowl, combine 1 cup of the brown sugar, 3 tablespoons of the cocoa powder, the flour, soy milk, olive oil, baking powder, sea salt, and vanilla extract.

2. Spread the mixture across the bottom of the slow cooker.

3. In a medium bowl, combine the remaining ¾ cup brown sugar and remaining ¼ cup cocoa powder.

4. Sprinkle the brown sugar and cocoa powder mixture over the batter in the slow cooker.

5. Pour the boiling water over the top of the mixture and the batter. Do not stir.

6. Cover and cook on high for 2 to 3 hours.

7. Insert a knife into the center of the brownies; if it comes out clean, your brownies are ready.

8. Serve hot with the vanilla soy ice cream, if desired.

Cherry Pie Drop Cake

MAKES 6 SERVINGS

Cherries are what make this pie-cake combo such a delight. When you feel like celebrating, serve this dessert with vanilla or chocolate soy ice cream and nondairy whipped topping for an extra treat.

1 (20-OUNCE) CAN CHERRY PIE FILLING
1 BOX VEGAN YELLOW CAKE MIX
½ CUP VEGAN MARGARINE, MELTED

1. Pour the cherry pie filling into the slow cooker.

2. In a medium bowl, combine the vegan margarine and the cake mix. Stir vigorously.

3. Drop the mixture over the pie filling.

4. Cover and cook on low for 3 hours.

5. Serve.

Pear and Chocolate Cake

MAKES 6 SERVINGS

Pears make this chocolate cake both delicious and highly nutritious. Fruit in general provides us with myriad health benefits, but pears surpass many other fruits when it comes to their phytonutrient (plant nutrient) and fiber content. Phytonutrients decrease inflammation and minimize free radicals in the body, both of which are associated with an increased risk of many forms of chronic disease, including heart disease, cancer, and diabetes. Pears are also easy to digest. This cake is best prepared in a smaller slow cooker.

NONSTICK COOKING SPRAY

1 (28-OUNCE) CAN PEAR HALVES IN SYRUP, DRAINED, ¼ CUP
   SYRUP RESERVED

¾ CUP ALL-PURPOSE FLOUR

½ CUP PLUS 2 TABLESPOONS PACKED LIGHT BROWN SUGAR

1 TEASPOON BAKING POWDER

¼ TEASPOON BAKING SODA

⅛ TEASPOON SEA SALT

½ CUP WATER

½ TEASPOON APPLE CIDER VINEGAR

¼ CUP UNSWEETENED COCOA POWDER

2 TABLESPOONS VEGAN MARGARINE

½ TEASPOON VANILLA EXTRACT

1. Lightly spray the slow cooker with the nonstick cooking spray.

2. Arrange the pears in the bottom of the slow cooker.

3. In a large bowl sift together the flour, $\frac{1}{2}$ cup of the brown sugar, the baking powder, baking soda, and sea salt.

4. In a large bowl whisk together the water, apple cider vinegar, cocoa powder, reserved pear syrup, and remaining 2 tablespoons brown sugar.

5. Add the vegan margarine to the cocoa powder mixture and heat in the microwave on high power for 3 minutes, or until boiling.

6. Remove the cocoa mixture from the microwave and whisk until smooth.

7. Stir the cocoa mixture into the flour mixture.

8. Add the vanilla extract.

9. Spread the batter over the pears in the slow cooker.

10. Cover and cook on low for 4 to 6 hours.

11. Remove the lid and let cool for 15 minutes.

12. Scoop out the cake onto dessert plates, placing the pears on top.

Chocolate–Peanut Butter Cake

MAKES 8 SERVINGS

Chocolate–Peanut Butter Cake in a slow cooker? Life is good. Chocolate and peanut butter have been a winning combination since Harry Burnett Reese invented Reese's Peanut Butter Cups in 1928. Harry didn't cater to the vegan, but this cake does. Serve a slice to your unsuspecting guests with your favorite nondairy frozen dessert.

FOR THE CHOCOLATE LAYER:

NONSTICK COOKING SPRAY

1 CUP ALL-PURPOSE FLOUR

½ CUP SUGAR

2 TABLESPOONS UNSWEETENED COCOA POWDER

1½ TEASPOONS BAKING POWDER

½ CUP UNSWEETENED SOY MILK

2 TABLESPOONS VEGAN MARGARINE, MELTED

1 TEASPOON VANILLA EXTRACT

¾ CUP VEGAN CHOCOLATE CHIPS

FOR THE PEANUT BUTTER LAYER:

¾ CUP SUGAR

¼ CUP UNSWEETENED COCOA POWDER

1 CUP BOILING WATER

½ CUP NATURAL PEANUT BUTTER

Make the chocolate layer:

1. Lightly spray the slow cooker with the nonstick cooking spray.

2. In a large bowl, combine the flour, sugar, cocoa powder, and baking powder.

3. Add the soy milk, vegan margarine, and vanilla. Stir until smooth.

4. Add the chocolate chips and pour into the slow cooker.

Make the peanut butter layer:

1. In a medium bowl, combine the sugar and cocoa powder.

2. In a small bowl, combine the boiling water and peanut butter.

3. Stir the peanut butter mixture into the cocoa mixture.

4. Pour the combined mixture evenly over the batter in the slow cooker.

5. Cover and cook on high for 2 to 2½ hours, or until a knife inserted into the center comes out clean.

6. Cool slightly before serving.

Nontraditional Brown Betty

MAKES 4 SERVINGS

Brown Betty is a traditional American dessert that has been around since at least the mid-1800s. Typically the Brown Betty is composed of fruit, usually apples, and some sort of breading layered to maximize flavor. This Nontraditional Brown Betty is made with bananas, pecans, and brandy or rum for a whole new flavor profile.

NONSTICK COOKING SPRAY

⅓ CUP MAPLE SYRUP

¼ CUP UNSWEETENED ALMOND MILK

½ TEASPOON GROUND CINNAMON

¼ TEASPOON GROUND GINGER

¼ TEASPOON GROUND NUTMEG

⅛ TEASPOON SEA SALT

6 CUPS CUBED WHITE BREAD

4 RIPE BANANAS, PEELED AND CHOPPED

⅓ CUP CHOPPED TOASTED PECANS

⅓ CUP PACKED LIGHT BROWN SUGAR

2 TABLESPOONS BRANDY OR RUM OR 1 TEASPOON BRANDY
    OR RUM EXTRACT

VANILLA NONDAIRY DESSERT (OPTIONAL)

1. Lightly spray the slow cooker with the nonstick cooking spray.

2. In a large bowl, combine the maple syrup, almond milk, cinnamon, ginger, nutmeg, and sea salt and mix well.

3. Add the bread cubes and stir to coat.

4. In a separate large bowl, combine the bananas, pecans, brown sugar, and your preference of alcohol or alcohol extract, stirring to mix.

5. Spread half of the bread mixture in the bottom of the cooker, followed by half of the banana mixture.

6. Repeat the layers.

7. Cover and cook on high for 1½ to 2 hours, or until firm.

8. Serve hot with a vanilla nondairy dessert, if desired.

Index

Acorn squash
  Sweet Acorn Squash, 53–54
  Vegan Risotto, 145
Adobo sauce, Mexican Beans
  and Rice, 131
All-purpose flour, as
  thickener, 10
Almond butter, Tempeh with
  Almond Butter, 184
Almond milk, Hash-Brown
  Casserole, 41
Almonds
  butter. *See* Almond butter
  Curried Almonds, 49
  milk. *See* Almond milk
  Super-Slow Tart Apple and
  Cinnamon Oatmeal, 39
Alphabet Minestrone, 2,
  75–76
Amaranth and Fruit, 35
Antipasto, Nontraditional
  Antipasto, 61–62
Apple cider
  Classic Apple Cobbler, 228
  Sweet Acorn Squash, 53–54
  vinegar. *See* Apple
  cider vinegar
Apple cider vinegar
  Barbecue-Style Tofu and
  Pineapple, 180–181
  Pear and Chocolate
  Cake, 232–233
  Pearl Barley and Lentil
  Soup, 88–89
  Rutabaga and Cabbage
  Stew, 165–166
  Tofu-Free Sloppy Joes, 200
Apple juice
  Apples and Cabbage, 155
  Sweet Acorn Squash, 53–54
Apples
  Apples and Cabbage, 155
  cider. *See* Apple cider

cider vinegar. *See* Apple
  cider vinegar
Home-Style Applesauce, 48
juice. *See* Apple juice
Slow-Baked Apples, 227
Super-Slow Tart Apple and
  Cinnamon Oatmeal, 39
Sweet Potato and Apple
  Curry, 218–219
Apricots
  Apricot Butter, 47
  Grains with Sesame
  Seeds, 136
  Rice Pudding, 226
  Root Vegetables and
  Dried Fruit, 158
  Sweetened Fruit Curry,
  217
Arborio rice. *See also* Rice
  preparation tips for, 23–24
  Root Vegetables and
  Dried Fruit, 158
  Vegan Risotto, 145
Arrowroot, as thickener, 10
Artichokes
  Nontraditional
  Antipasto, 61–62
  Spinach and Yellow
  Rice, 129
Asian chili sauce, 67
Asian-style dishes
  Asian Fall Vegetable
  Stew, 208
  Asian Potato Salad, 203
  "Chicken" Chow Mein, 209
  Chinese Hot Pot, 206–207
  Hot and Sour Soup, 67
Asian-styled dishes
  Vietnamese Noodle
  Soup, 204–205
Avocado
  Black Bean and Chipotle
  Pepper Stew, 107

Black Bean Breakfast
  Burritos, 2, 25, 42–43
  Mexican Rice with Black
  Beans and Salsa, 211–212

B
Baby carrots. *See also* Carrots
  Chunky Seitan Roast, 192
  Hot and Sour Soup, 67
  Jamaican Red Bean Soup, 95
  Mandarin Orange
  Vegetables and Rice, 128
Baby lima beans, Lima Bean
  Chili, 117–118
Baby spinach, Polenta and
  Bean Casserole, 168–169
Baked Bean Chili, 116
Balsamic vinegar
  Root Vegetables with
  Oil and Vinegar, 52
  Who Needs Meat
  Meat Sauce, 198
Bamboo shoots, Hot and Sour
  Soup, 67
Banana Quinoa Breakfast, 34
Barbecue-Style Tofu and
  Pineapple, 180–181
Barley
  Barley and Beans, 134
  Kidney Bean and Barley
  Stuffed Squash, 163
  pearl. *See* Pearl barley
Basil pesto, Polenta and Bean
  Casserole, 168–169
Basmati rice. *See also* Rice
  Cajun-Style Kidney
  Beans and Rice, 132
  "Chicken" Chow Mein, 209
  Chickpea Coconut
  Curry, 220
  Chinese Hot Pot, 206–207
  Crispy Tofu and Brown
  Basmati Rice, 178–179

Basmati rice. (*continued*)
  Cruciferous Vegetables,
    Tofu, and Rice, 177
  Kidney Bean Curry and
    Basmati Rice, 221
  Mandarin Orange
    Vegetables and Rice, 128
  Mexican Beans
    and Rice, 131
  Slow-Cooked Brown
    Basmati Rice, 22–23
Bean curd. *See* Tofu
Bean sprouts
  Asian Potato Salad, 203
  "Chicken" Chow Mein, 209
  Vietnamese Noodle
    Soup, 204–205
Beans, 125–149
  Baked Bean Chili, 116
  Barley and Beans, 134
  Bean and Penne
    Soup, 93–94
  Bean Smorgasbord, 138
  Beans and Molasses, 135
  Beans, Beans, and More
    Beans Soup, 92
  black. *See* Black beans
  cannellini. *See*
    Cannellini beans
  conversion formulas
    for, 25–26
  cook times for, 26
  Great Northern Bean
    "Chicken" Chili, 124
  green. *See* Green beans
  kidney. *See* Kidney beans
  Lentil and Bean
    Stew, 108–109
  lima. *See* Lima beans
  Lima Bean Gumbo, 149
  Mexican Bean Dip, 63
  Mom's Vegetable
    Soup, 73–74
  mung. *See* Mung beans
  Old-Fashioned Beans
    and Weenies, 199
  pinto. *See* Pinto beans
  Polenta and Bean
    Casserole, 168–169
  red. *See* Red beans
  shortcuts for, 19, 25–27
  Slow-Cooked Beans, 26–27

  soaking process for, 26
  Southern-Style
    Casserole, 147–148
  white. *See* White beans
Bell peppers
  Baked Bean Chili, 116
  Bean and Penne
    Soup, 93–94
  Black Bean and Chipotle
    Pepper Stew, 107
  Black Bean Soup, 85
  Carrot and Green Bean
    Casserole, 170
  Creamy Curry Stew,
    103–104
  Crispy Tofu and Brown
    Basmati Rice, 178–179
  green. *See* Green
    bell peppers
  Italian Oyster Mushrooms
    and Pilaf, 162
  Lima Bean Chili, 117–118
  Lima Bean Gumbo, 149
  Mom's Vegetable
    Soup, 73–74
  Nontraditional
    Antipasto, 61–62
  preparation tips for, 11
  Quinoa Chili, 121–122
  Rataouille Niçoise, 2, 157
  red. *See* Red bell peppers
  Spinach and Yellow
    Rice, 129
  Stuffed Bell Peppers, 196
  Stuffed Picante Onions, 55
  Sweet Potato Chili, 120
  Tempeh and Tofu
    Hungarian Goulash,
    190–191
  Tofu-Free Sloppy Joes, 200
  Two-Bean Chili, 113
  yellow. *See* Yellow
    bell peppers
Black beans
  Bean Smorgasbord, 138
  Black Bean and Chipotle
    Pepper Stew, 107
  Black Bean and
    Tomato Chili, 114
  Black Bean Breakfast
    Burritos, 2, 25, 42–43
  Black Bean Soup, 85

  Black Bean Tacos, 214
  cook times for, 26
  Greens, Greens, Greens, 153
  Lima Bean Chili, 117–118
  Mexican Bean Dip, 63
  Mexican Rice with Black
    Beans and Salsa, 211–212
  Mexican-Style Dumpling
    Stew, 110–111
  Mexican-Style
    Lasagna, 215–216
  Mexican-Style
    Minestrone, 210
  Quinoa Chili, 121–122
  Spanish Rice and
    Black Beans, 130
  Spicy Vegan Chili, 119
  Sweet Potato Chili, 120
  Tempeh Enchilada
    Casserole, 187–188
Black olives, Tempeh
  Enchilada Casserole,
  187–188
Black-eyed peas
  Bean Smorgasbord, 138
  Black-Eyed Pea Chili, 115
  cook times for, 26
  Mexican Black-
    Eyed Peas, 137
Blackstrap molasses, Beans
  and Molasses, 135
Bok choy, Cruciferous
  Vegetables, Tofu, and
  Rice, 177
Brandy, Nontraditional
  Brown Betty, 236–237
Bread crumbs, Slow-Cooked
  Stuffing, 140
Breakfasts, 29–43
  Amaranth and Fruit, 35
  Banana Quinoa
    Breakfast, 34
  Black Bean Breakfast
    Burritos, 2, 25, 42–43
  Chocolaty Steel-
    Cut Oats, 40
  Coconutty Oats, 38
  Extra-Creamy Tapioca
    Pudding, 33
  Hash-Brown Casserole, 41
  Pumpkin Cinnamon
    Rolls, 2, 31–32

Pumpkin Gingerbread
    Cereal, 36–37
Super-Slow Tart Apple and
    Cinnamon Oatmeal, 39
Broccoli
    Crispy Tofu and Brown
        Basmati Rice, 178–179
    Fettuccine and
        Vegetables, 174
    Mac and Cheese, 142
    Mandarin Orange
        Vegetables and Rice, 128
    Sweet and Spicy
        Chickpea Stew, 102
Broth, vegetable
    bouillon cubes, 20–22
    definition of, 20
    preparation instructions
        for, 21–22
    shortcuts for, 19
    vs. stock, 19–20.
Brown rice. See also Rice
    Beans and Molasses, 135
    Cajun-Style Kidney
        Beans and Rice, 132
    "Chicken" Chow Mein, 209
    Chickpea Coconut
        Curry, 220
    Chinese Hot Pot, 206–207
    Crispy Tofu and Brown
        Basmati Rice, 178–179
    Cruciferous Vegetables,
        Tofu, and Rice, 177
    Drunken "Chicken" with
        Brown Rice, 197
    Kidney Bean Curry and
        Basmati Rice, 221
    Mandarin Orange
        Vegetables and Rice, 128
    Mexican Beans
        and Rice, 131
    Slow-Cooked Brown
        Basmati Rice, 22–23
    Spanish Rice and
        Black Beans, 130
    Stuffed Bell Peppers, 196
Brown sugar
    Banana Quinoa
        Breakfast, 34
    Beans and Molasses, 135
    Butterscotch Sauce, 225
    dark. See Dark brown sugar

Fudgy Brownies, 230
    light. See Light brown sugar
Pear and Chocolate
    Cake, 232–233
Pumpkin Pie, 229
Root Vegetables with
    Oil and Vinegar, 52
Slow-Baked Apples, 227
Super-Slow Tart Apple and
    Cinnamon Oatmeal, 39
Sweet Acorn Squash,
    53–54
Sweet Potato Casserole,
    56
Brownies, Fudgy Brownies,
    230
Bulgar wheat, Grains with
    Sesame Seeds, 136
Boullion cubes, vegetable, 19
Burritos, Black Bean
    Breakfast Burritos, 2, 25,
    42–43
Butternut squash
    Coconut, Squash, and
        Tofu Soup, 82
    Creamy Butternut
        Squash Soup, 71–72
    Eggplant, Okra, and
        Butternut Squash
        Stew, 167
    Peanut, Tempeh,
        and Butternut
        Squash, 185–186
    Veggie and Squash
        Stew, 106
Butters
    almond, Tempeh with
        Almond Butter, 184
    Apricot Butter, 47
    cashew, Hearty Stew, 195
    peanut. See Peanut butter
Butterscotch Sauce, 225

C
Cabbage
    Apples and Cabbage, 155
    Cruciferous Vegetables,
        Tofu, and Rice, 177
    Rutabaga and Cabbage
        Stew, 165–166
    Sweet Potato and Apple
        Curry, 218–219

Cajun-Style Kidney Beans
    and Rice, 132
Cakes
    Cherry Pie Drop Cake, 231
    Chocolate–Peanut Butter
        Cake, 2, 234–235
    Pear and Chocolate
        Cake, 232–233
Cannellini beans
    cook times for, 26
    Polenta and Bean
        Casserole, 168–169
Capers, Eggplant and Capers,
    156
Carnival squash, Kidney
    Bean and Barley Stuffed
    Squash, 163
Carrots
    Alphabet Minestrone,
        2, 75–76
    baby. See Baby carrots
    Bean and Penne Soup, 93–94
    Carrot and Green Bean
        Casserole, 170
    "Chicken" Chow Mein, 209
    Chickpea Coconut
        Curry, 220
    Chunky Seitan Roast, 192
    Classic Veggies
        and Rice, 161
    Coconut, Squash, and
        Tofu Soup, 82
    Creamy Chickpea
        Soup, 80–81
    Crispy Tofu and Brown
        Basmati Rice, 178–179
    Drunken "Chicken" with
        Brown Rice, 197
    Easy Millet Stew, 101
    Eggplant, Okra, and
        Butternut Squash
        Stew, 167
    Frozen Veggie Stew, 99–100
    Hearty Stew, 195
    Hot and Sour Soup, 67
    Italian Roasted Veggies, 154
    Jamaican Red Bean
        Soup, 95
    Lentil and Bean
        Stew, 108–109
    Lentil and Mushroom
        Soup, 87

Carrots (*continued*)
Lentil Pasta Sauce, 141
Mandarin Orange
Vegetables and Rice, 128
"Meaty" Shiitake Stew, 112
Mexican-Style Dumpling
Stew, 110–111
Mom's Vegetable
Soup, 73–74
Moroccan-Style Lentil
Soup, 90–91
Nontraditional
Antipasto, 61–62
Old-Fashioned Split
Pea Soup, 69
Pearl Barley and Lentil
Soup, 88–89
Portobello Mushroom and
Tempeh Stroganoff, 189
Root Vegetables and
Dried Fruit, 158
Root Vegetables with
Oil and Vinegar, 52
Rutabaga and Cabbage
Stew, 165–166
Seitan and Sausage
Cassoulet, 194
Spaghetti and Hot Dogs, 146
Sweet and Spicy
Chickpea Stew, 102
Sweet Potato and Apple
Curry, 218–219
Two-Bean Chili, 113
Veggie and Chickpea
Soup, 77–78
Veggie and Lentil Soup, 86
Veggie and Squash
Stew, 106
Vietnamese Noodle
Soup, 204–205
Cashew butter, Hearty Stew,
195
Cashews
butter. *See* Cashew butter
Macaroni Casserole
Florentine, 143–144
Nutty Coconut
Curry Mix, 51
Casseroles
Carrot and Green Bean
Casserole, 170
Hash-Brown Casserole, 41

Macaroni Casserole
Florentine, 143–144
Polenta and Bean
Casserole, 168–169
Southern-Style
Casserole, 147–148
Sweet Potato Casserole, 56
Tempeh Enchilada
Casserole, 2, 187–188
Cauliflower
"Cheesy" Cauliflower, 164
Chickpea Coconut
Curry, 220
Creamy Curry Stew,
103–104
A Little More than
Split Pea Soup, 70
Mashed Cauliflower and
Garlic "Potatoes," 2, 57
Cayenne pepper
Bean and Penne
Soup, 93–94
Black Bean Breakfast
Burritos, 2, 25, 42–43
Black Bean Tacos, 214
Chickpea Couscous, 133
Creamy Pumpkin Stew,
105
Great Northern Bean
"Chicken" Chili, 124
Mac and Cheese, 142
Moroccan-Style Lentil
Soup, 90–91
Stuffed Picante Onions, 55
Sweet and Spicy
Chickpea Stew, 102
Tofu-Free Sloppy Joes, 200
Celery stalks
Alphabet Minestrone,
2, 75–76
Asian Potato Salad, 203
Barley and Beans, 134
Bean and Penne
Soup, 93–94
Carrot and Green Bean
Casserole, 170
"Chicken" Chow Mein, 209
Chinese Hot Pot, 206–207
Coconut, Squash, and
Tofu Soup, 82
Creamy Baked Potato
and Veggie Soup, 96

Creamy Chickpea
Soup, 80–81
Cruciferous Vegetables,
Tofu, and Rice, 177
Easy Millet Stew, 101
Eggplant and Capers, 156
Frozen Veggie Stew, 99–100
Lentil and Mushroom
Soup, 87
Lentil Pasta Sauce, 141
A Little More than
Split Pea Soup, 70
Mom's Vegetable
Soup, 73–74
Moroccan-Style Lentil
Soup, 90–91
Old-Fashioned Split
Pea Soup, 69
Pearl Barley and Lentil
Soup, 88–89
Portobello Mushroom and
Tempeh Stroganoff, 189
Quinoa Chili, 121–122
Rutabaga and Cabbage
Stew, 165–166
Slow-Cooked Stuffing, 140
Sweet and Spicy
Chickpea Stew, 102
Sweet Potato and Apple
Curry, 218–219
Veggie and Lentil Soup, 86
Cereal
Pumpkin Gingerbread
Cereal, 36–37
rice, Nutty Coconut
Curry Mix, 51
Cheddar cheese, vegan
Black Bean and
Tomato Chili, 114
Black Bean Breakfast
Burritos, 2, 25, 42–43
"Cheesy" Cauliflower, 164
"Cheesy" Zucchini, Leeks,
and Tomatoes, 159–160
Creamy Baked Potato
and Veggie Soup, 96
Cheese, vegan
Black Bean and
Tomato Chili, 114
Black Bean Breakfast
Burritos, 2, 25, 42–43
"Cheesy" Cauliflower, 164

"Cheesy" Zucchini, Leeks,
and Tomatoes, 159–160
Creamy Baked Potato
and Veggie Soup, 96
"Cheesy" Cauliflower, 164
"Cheesy" Zucchini, Leeks,
and Tomatoes, 159–160
Cherries
Cherry Pie Drop Cake, 231
Grains with Sesame
Seeds, 136
Rice Pudding, 226
Chicken, vegan
"Chicken" Chow Mein, 209
Drunken "Chicken" with
Brown Rice, 197
Great Northern Bean
"Chicken" Chili, 124
Mexican-Style
Lasagna, 215–216
Chickpeas
Baked Bean Chili, 116
Chickpea Coconut
Curry, 220
Chickpea Couscous, 133
cook times for, 26
Creamy Chickpea
Soup, 80–81
Creamy Curry Stew,
103–104
green. See Green chickpeas
Lentil and Bean
Stew, 108–109
Moroccan-Style Lentil
Soup, 90–91
Polenta and Bean
Casserole, 168–169
Spiced Indian
Chickpeas, 60
Sweet and Spicy
Chickpea Stew, 102
Veggie and Chickpea
Soup, 77–78
Veggie and Squash
Stew, 106
Chiles
Black Bean Breakfast
Burritos, 2, 25, 42–43
green. See Green chiles
Mexican Bean Dip, 63
Mexican-Style Dumpling
Stew, 110–111

red. See Red chiles
Spiced Indian
Chickpeas, 60
Chili beans, Beans and
Molasses, 135
Chilies and stews, 97–124
Asian Fall Vegetable
Stew, 208
Baked Bean Chili, 116
Black Bean and Chipotle
Pepper Stew, 107
Black Bean and
Tomato Chili, 114
Black-Eyed Pea Chili, 115
Creamy Curry Stew,
103–104
Creamy Pumpkin Stew, 105
Easy Millet Stew, 101
Frozen Veggie Stew, 99–100
Great Northern Bean
"Chicken" Chili, 124
Hearty Stew, 195
Lentil and Bean
Stew, 108–109
Lima Bean Chili, 117–118
"Meaty" Shiitake
Stew, 2, 112
Mexican-Style Dumpling
Stew, 110–111
Quinoa Chili, 121–122
Rutabaga and Cabbage
Stew, 165–166
Spicy Pumpkin Chili, 123
Spicy Vegan Chili, 119
Sweet and Spicy
Chickpea Stew, 102
Sweet Potato Chili, 120
Two-Bean Chili, 113
Veggie and Squash
Stew, 106
Chinese Hot Pot, 206–207
Chipotle peppers
Black Bean and Chipotle
Pepper Stew, 107
Black Beans Tacos, 214
Creamy Chickpea
Soup, 80–81
Mexican Beans
and Rice, 131
Chocolate, vegan
Chocolate-Peanut Butter
Cake, 2, 234–235

Chocolaty Steel-Cut Oats, 40
Chow mein, "Chicken" Chow
Mein, 209
Chunky Seitan Roast, 192
Cider, Sweet Acorn Squash,
53–54
Cider vinegar, Pearl Barley
and Lentil Soup, 88–89
Cilantro
Asian Fall Vegetable
Stew, 208
Black Bean and Chipotle
Pepper Stew, 107
Black Bean and
Tomato Chili, 114
Black Bean Breakfast
Burritos, 2, 25, 42–43
Coconut, Squash, and
Tofu Soup, 82
Creamy Curry Stew,
103–104
Lima Bean Chili, 117–118
Meaty Seitan Tacos, 193
Mexican Rice with Black
Beans and Salsa, 211–212
Root Vegetables and
Dried Fruit, 158
Spiced Indian
Chickpeas, 60
Spicy Vegan Chili, 119
Split Mung Bean
Soup, 83–84
Tomato Salsa, 58
Two-Bean Chili, 113
Cinnamon
Apricot Butter, 47
Banana Quinoa
Breakfast, 34
Black Bean and Chipotle
Pepper Stew, 107
Classic Apple Cobbler, 228
Home-Style Applesauce, 48
Moroccan-Style Lentil
Soup, 90–91
Nontraditional Brown
Betty, 236–237
Peanut, Tempeh, and
Butternut Squash
Mole, 185–186
Pumpkin Cinnamon
Rolls, 2, 31–32
Rice Pudding, 226

Cinnamon (*continued*)
Root Vegetables and
Dried Fruit, 158
Slow-Baked Apples, 227
Spicy Pecans, 50
Super-Slow Tart Apple and
Cinnamon Oatmeal, 39
Sweet Acorn Squash, 53–54
Vietnamese Noodle
Soup, 204–205
Classic Veggies and Rice, 161
Cobblers, Classic Apple
Cobbler, 228
Cocoa powder, unsweetened
Black Bean and
Tomato Chili, 114
Chocolate–Peanut Butter
Cake, 2, 234–235
Chocolaty Steel-
Cut Oats, 40
Fudgy Brownies, 230
Pear and Chocolate
Cake, 232–233
Sweet Potato Chili, 120
Coconut milk, unsweetened
Asian Fall Vegetable
Stew, 208
Chickpea Coconut
Curry, 220
Chocolaty Steel-
Cut Oats, 40
Coconut, Squash, and
Tofu Soup, 82
Coconutty Oats, 38
Creamy Curry Stew,
103–104
Creamy Pumpkin Stew, 105
Extra-Creamy Tapioca
Pudding, 33
Fettuccine and
Vegetables, 174
Jamaican Red Bean Soup, 95
Sweet Potato and Apple
Curry, 218–219
Coconuts
Coconut, Squash, and
Tofu Soup, 82
Coconutty Oats, 38
creamer, Butterscotch
Sauce, 225
milk. *See* Coconut milk,
unsweetened

Nutty Coconut
Curry Mix, 51
Collards, Greens, Greens,
Greens, 153
Converted rice, 23. *See also*
Rice
Curried Rice and
Lentils, 222
Drunken "Chicken" with
Brown Rice, 197
Enchilada Wraps, 2, 213
Cookers, slow. *See* Slow
cookers
Cooking sprays. *See* Nonstick
cooking sprays
Corn
Beans, Beans, and More
Beans Soup, 92
Black Bean Breakfast
Burritos, 2, 25, 42–43
Black Beans Tacos, 214
Black-Eyed Pea Chili, 115
creamed. *See* Creamed corn
Creamy Pumpkin Stew, 105
Frozen Veggie Stew, 99–100
Lentil and Bean
Stew, 108–109
Lima Bean Gumbo, 149
Mexican-Style Dumpling
Stew, 110–111
Mexican-Style
Lasagna, 215–216
Mexican-Style
Minestrone, 210
Southern-Style
Casserole, 147–148
Tempeh Enchilada
Casserole, 187–188
Veggie Bake, 173
Cornstarch, as thickener, 10
Couscous
Chickpea Couscous, 133
Veggie and Squash
Stew, 106
Cranberries
Grains with Sesame
Seeds, 136
Rice Pudding, 226
Slow-Baked Apples, 227
Super-Slow Tart Apple and
Cinnamon Oatmeal, 39
Cream cheese (vegan),

Pumpkin Cinnamon
Rolls, 31–32
Creamed corn
Southern-Style
Casserole, 147–148
Veggie Bake, 173
Creamy Baked Potato and
Veggie Soup, 96
Creamy Butternut Squash
Soup, 71–72
Creamy Chickpea Soup, 80–81
Creamy Curry Stew, 103–104
Creamy Pumpkin Stew, 105
Crispy Tofu and Brown
Basmati Rice, 178–179
Crookneck squash, Rataouille
Niçoise, 2, 157
Cruciferous Vegetables, Tofu,
and Rice, 177
Crumbles, soy
Stuffed Bell Peppers, 196
Who Needs Meat
Meat Sauce, 198
Curd, bean. *See* Tofu
Curried Almonds, 49
Curried Rice and Lentils, 222
Curry powder
Chickpea Coconut
Curry, 220
Creamy Curry Stew, 103–104
Curried Almonds, 49
Curried Rice and
Lentils, 222
Kidney Bean Curry and
Basmati Rice, 221
Nutty Coconut
Curry Mix, 51
Sweet Potato and Apple
Curry, 218–219
Sweetened Fruit Curry, 217

D
Dark brown sugar, Super-
Slow Tart Apple and
Cinnamon Oatmeal, 39
Dates
Amaranth and Fruit, 35
Barbecue-Style Tofu and
Pineapple, 180–181
Desserts, 223–237
Butterscotch Sauce, 225
Cherry Pie Drop Cake, 231

"Chicken" Chow Mein, 209
Chocolate–Peanut Butter
    Cake, 234–235
Classic Apple Cobbler, 228
Fudgy Brownies, 230
Nontraditional Brown
    Betty, 236–237
Pear and Chocolate
    Cake, 232–233
Pumpkin Pie, 229
Rice Pudding, 226
Slow-Baked Apples, 227
Dips, Mexican Bean Dip, 63
Dried fruit, Root Vegetables
    and Dried Fruit, 158
Dried *vs.* fresh herbs, 11. *See
    also* Herbs
Drunken "Chicken" with
    Brown Rice, 197
Dumplings, Mexican-Style
    Dumpling Stew, 110–111

E
Easy Millet Stew, 101
Egg substitutes
    Pumpkin Cinnamon
        Rolls, 31–32
    Pumpkin Pie, 229
    Southern-Style
        Casserole, 147–148
    Sweet Potato Casserole, 56
Eggplant
    Eggplant and Capers, 156
    Eggplant, Okra, and
        Butternut Squash
        Stew, 167
    Eggplant Parmesan, 172
    Ratatouille Niçoise, 2, 157
Elbow pasta. *See also* Pastas
    Mac and Cheese, 142
    Macaroni Casserole
        Florentine, 143–144
    Tempeh and Tofu Hungarian
        Goulash, 190–191
Enchiladas
    Enchilada Wraps, 2, 213
    Tempeh Enchilada
        Casserole, 2, 187–188
Equivalents, eggs. *See* Egg
    substitutes
Extra-Creamy Tapioca
    Pudding, 33

F
Farro and Split Pea Soup, 127
Fat, as thickener, 10
Fennel bulb, Nontraditional
    Antipasto, 61–62
Feta cheese, vegan
    Ratatouille Niçoise, 2, 157
    Veggie and Squash
        Stew, 106
Fettuccine and Vegetables,
    174
Fifteen-bean soup mix, Beans,
    Beans, and More Beans
    Soup, 92
Flaxseed
    Pumpkin Gingerbread
        Cereal, 36–37
    Super-Slow Tart Apple and
        Cinnamon Oatmeal, 39
Flour, as thickener, 10
Fresh ginger
    Chinese Hot Pot, 206–207
    Creamy Butternut
        Squash Soup, 71–72
    Creamy Curry Stew,
        103–104
    Hot and Sour Soup, 67
    Mandarin Orange
        Vegetables and Rice, 128
    Moroccan-Style Lentil
        Soup, 90–91
    Spices Indian Chickpeas, 60
    Vietnamese Noodle
        Soup, 204–205
Fresh *vs.* dried herbs, 11
Frozen Veggie Stew, 99–100
Fruit
    Amaranth and Fruit, 35
    Root Vegetables and
        Dried Fruit, 158
    Sweetened Fruit Curry, 217

G
Garam masala
    Farro and Split Pea
        Soup, 127
    Moroccan-Style Lentil
        Soup, 90–91
Garlic
    Barbecue-Style Tofu and
        Pineapple, 180–181

Bean and Penne
    Soup, 93–94
Beans, Beans, and More
    Beans Soup, 92
Creamy Baked Potato
    and Veggie Soup, 96
Creamy Butternut
    Squash Soup, 71–72
Creamy Pumpkin Stew, 105
Garlicky Tomato Soup, 68
Hot and Sour Soup, 67
Mashed Cauliflower and
    Garlic "Potatoes," 2, 57
Meaty Seitan Tacos, 193
Mexican Beans
    and Rice, 131
Mom's Vegetable
    Soup, 73–74
Nontraditional
    Antipasto, 61–62
precooking of, 11
Quinoa Chili, 121–122
Tofu-Free Sloppy Joes, 200
Veggie and Lentil Soup, 86
Garlicky Tomato Soup, 68
Ginger, fresh
    Chinese Hot Pot, 206–207
    Creamy Butternut
        Squash Soup, 71–72
    Creamy Curry Stew,
        103–104
    Hot and Sour Soup, 67
    Mandarin Orange
        Vegetables and Rice, 128
    Moroccan-Style Lentil
        Soup, 90–91
    Spiced Indian
        Chickpeas, 60
    Vietnamese Noodle
        Soup, 204–205
Gingerbread, Pumpkin
    Gingerbread Cereal,
    36–37
Grain dishes, 125–149
    Barley and Beans, 134
    Bean Smorgasbord, 138
    Beans and Molasses, 135
    black-eyed peas. *See*
        Black-eyed peas
    couscous. *See* Couscous
    Farro and Split Pea
        Soup, 127

Grain dishes (*continued*)
Grains with Sesame
Seeds, 136
Lentil Pasta Sauce, 141
lentils. *See* Lentils
Lima Bean Gumbo, 149
Mac and Cheese, 142
Macaroni Casserole
Florentine, 143–144
Mexican Black-
Eyed Peas, 137
pastas. *See* Pastas
rice. *See* Rice
Slow-Cooked Stuffing, 140
Southern-Style
Casserole, 147–148
Spaghetti and Hot Dogs, 146
Spicy Lentils, 139
Vegan Risotto, 145
Veggie and Squash
Stew, 106
Great northern beans
Bean Smorgasbord, 138
cook times for, 26
Great Northern Bean
"Chicken" Chili, 124
Old-Fashioned Beans
and Weenies, 199
Green beans
Alphabet Minestrone,
2, 75–76
Bean and Penne
Soup, 93–94
Carrot and Green Bean
Casserole, 170
Chickpea Coconut
Curry, 220
Mexican-Style
Minestrone, 210
Mom's Vegetable
Soup, 73–74
Veggie and Chickpea
Soup, 77–78
Veggie Bake, 173
Green bell peppers. *See also*
Bell peppers
Baked Bean Chili, 116
Black Bean and Chipotle
Pepper Stew, 107
Black Bean Soup, 85
Italian Oyster Mushrooms
and Pilaf, 162

Lima Bean Chili, 117–118
Lima Bean Gumbo, 149
Quinoa Chili, 121–122
Stuffed Bell Peppers, 196
Sweet Potato Chili, 120
Tofu Sloppy Joes, 182
Two-Bean Chili, 113
Who Needs Meat
Meat Sauce, 198
Green chickpeas, Lentil and
Bean Stew, 108–109
Green chiles. *See also* Chiles
Black Bean Breakfast
Burritos, 2, 25, 42–43
Mexican Bean Dip, 63
Mexican Rice with Black
Beans and Salsa,
211–212
Mexican-Style Dumpling
Stew, 110–111
Spicy Lentils, 139
Tempeh Enchilada
Casserole, 187–188
Two-Bean Chili, 113
Green olives, Eggplant and
Capers, 156
Greens, Greens, Greens, 153
Guacamole, Black Bean
Breakfast Burritos, 2, 25,
42–43

H
Hard vegetables, preparation
tips for, 11
Hash-Brown Casserole, 41
Hearty Stew, 195
Herbs
fresh *vs.* dried, 11
substitution of, 11
High altitude considerations,
15
Hoisin sauce, Vietnamese
Noodle Soup, 204–205
Home-Style Applesauce, 48
Horseradish, Sweet and Spicy
Chickpea Stew, 102
Hot and Sour Soup, 67
Hot dogs, vegan
Old-Fashioned Beans
and Weenies, 199
Spaghetti and Hot Dogs, 146

I
Ice cream (soy)
Fudgy Brownies, 230
Slow-Baked Apples, 227
Ice cream (soy), Slow-Baked
Apples, 227
Icing, Pumpkin Cinnamon
Rolls, 2, 31–32
International cuisine,
201–222
Asian Fall Vegetable
Stew, 208
Asian Potato Salad, 203
Asian-style dishes. *See*
Asian-style dishes
Black Bean Tacos, 214
Chickpea Coconut
Curry, 220
Chinese Hot Pot, 206–207
Curried Rice and
Lentils, 222
Enchilada Wraps, 2, 213
Kidney Bean Curry and
Basmati Rice, 221
Mexican Rice with Black
Beans and Salsa,
211–212
Mexican-Style
Lasagna, 215–216
Mexican-Style
Minestrone, 210
Sweet Potato and Apple
Curry, 218–219
Sweetened Fruit Curry, 217
Vietnamese Noodle
Soup, 204–205
Irish Oats, Chocolaty Steel-
Cut Oats, 40
Italian Roasted Veggies, 154

J
Jalepeño peppers
Bean and Penne
Soup, 93–94
Black Bean Soup, 85
Black-Eyed Pea Chili, 115
Lima Bean Chili, 117–118
Tomato Salsa, 58
Jamaican Red Bean Soup,
95

K

Kale, Greens, Greens, Greens,
153
Kidney beans
Alphabet Minestrone,
2, 75–76
Baked Bean Chili, 116
Barley and Beans, 134
Bean and Penne
Soup, 93–94
Beans and Molasses, 135
Cajun-Style Kidney
Beans and Rice, 132
cook times for, 26
Enchilada Wraps, 2, 213
Jamaican Red Bean Soup, 95
Kidney Bean and Barley
Stuffed Squash, 163
Kidney Beans Curry and
Basmati Rice, 221
Lima Bean Chili, 117–118
Mexican Bean Dip, 63
Mexican Beans
and Rice, 131
Mexican-Style Dumpling
Stew, 110–111
Quinoa Chili, 121–122
Southern-Style
Casserole, 147–148
Spicy Pumpkin Chili, 123
Sweet Potato Chili, 120
Two-Bean Chili, 113
Kombu seaweed
Rutabaga and Cabbage
Stew, 165–166
Veggie and Chickpea
Soup, 77–78

L

Lasagna
Mexican-Style
Lasagna, 215–216
Tofu and Spinach
Lasagna, 183
Leeks
"Cheesy" Zucchini, Leeks,
and Tomatoes, 159–160
Hearty Stew, 195
Lemon grass stalks, Coconut,
Squash, and Tofu Soup,
82

Lentils
cook times for, 26
Curried Rice and
Lentils, 222
Lentil and Bean
Stew, 108–109
Lentil and Mushroom
Soup, 87
Lentil Pasta Sauce, 141
Moroccan-Style Lentil
Soup, 90–91
Pearl Barley and Lentil
Soup, 88–89
Spicy Lentils, 139
Tofu-Free Sloppy Joes, 200
Veggie and Lentil Soup, 86
Lettuce
Asian Potato Salad, 203
Black Bean Breakfast
Burritos, 2, 25, 42–43
Black Beans Tacos, 214
Light brown sugar. *See also*
Brown sugar
Butterscotch Sauce, 225
Fudgy Brownies, 230
Pear and Chocolate
Cake, 232–233
Pumpkin Pie, 229
Root Vegetables with
Oil and Vinegar, 52
Slow-Baked Apples, 227
Sweet Acorn Squash, 53–54
Sweet Potato Casserole, 56
Lima beans
Lima Bean Chili, 117–118
Lima Bean Gumbo, 149
Liquid smoke, Cajun-Style
Kidney Beans and Rice,
132
Long-grain rice
Classic Veggies
and Rice, 161
Curried Rice and
Lentils, 222
Drunken "Chicken" with
Brown Rice, 197
Enchilada Wraps, 2, 213

M

Mac and Cheese, 142
Mandarin oranges

Asian Potato Salad, 203
Mandarin Orange
Vegetables and Rice, 128
Maple syrup
Chocolaty Steel-
Cut Oats, 40
Meaty Seitan Tacos, 193
Pumpkin Gingerbread
Cereal, 36–37
Sweet Acorn Squash, 53–54
Margarine, vegan
Banana Quinoa
Breakfast, 34
Cherry Pie Drop Cake, 231
Creamy Baked Potato
and Veggie Soup, 96
Curried Almonds, 49
Fettuccine and
Vegetables, 174
Marinated Mushrooms, 59
Mashed Cauliflower and
Garlic "Potatoes," 2, 57
Nutty Coconut
Curry Mix, 51
Pumpkin Cinnamon
Rolls, 31–32
Slow-Baked Apples, 227
Spicy Pecans, 50
Stuffed Picante Onions, 55
Marinated Mushrooms, 59
Mashed Cauliflower and
Garlic "Potatoes," 2, 57
Meat alternatives, 175–200
Drunken "Chicken" with
Brown Rice, 197
Hearty Stew, 195
Old-Fashioned Beans
and Weenies, 199
seitan. *See* Seitan
Stuffed Bell Peppers, 196
tempeh. *See* Tempeh
tofu. *See* Tofu
Tofu-Free Sloppy Joes, 200
Who Needs Meat
Meat Sauce, 198
"Meaty" Shiitake Stew, 2, 112
Mexican-styled dishes
Black Bean Tacos, 214
Enchilada Wraps, 2, 213
Meaty Seitan Tacos, 193
Mexican Bean Dip, 63

Mexican-styled
dishes (*continued*)
  Mexican Beans
    and Rice, 131
  Mexican Black-
    Eyed Peas, 137
  Mexican Rice with Black
    Beans and Salsa, 211–212
  Mexican-Style
    Lasagna, 215–216
  Mexican-Style
    Minestrone, 210
  salsas. *See* Salsas
  Tempeh Enchilada
    Casserole, 187–188
Millet, Easy Millet Stew, 101
Minestrone. *See also* Soups
  Alphabet Minestrone,
    2, 75–76
  Mexican-Style
    Minestrone, 210
Miso paste
  Macaroni Casserole
    Florentine, 143–144
  Vietnamese Noodle
    Soup, 204–205
Molasses, Beans and Molasses,
  135
Mom's Vegetable Soup,
  73–74
Moroccan-Style Lentil Soup,
  90–91
Mozzarella cheese, vegan
  Creamy Chickpea
    Soup, 80–81
  Fettuccine and
    Vegetables, 174
Mung beans, Split Mung Bean
  Soup, 83–84
Mushrooms
  Asian Fall Vegetable
    Stew, 208
  "Cheesy" Cauliflower, 164
  Chinese Hot Pot, 206–207
  Easy Millet Stew, 101
  Fettuccine and
    Vegetables, 174
  Hot and Sour Soup, 67
  Italian Oyster Mushrooms
    and Pilaf, 162
  Lentil and Bean
    Stew, 108–109

Lentil and Mushroom
  Soup, 87
Marinated Mushrooms, 59
"Meaty" Shiitake
  Stew, 2, 112
Nontraditional
  Antipasto, 61–62
Portobello Mushroom
  Submarine
  Sandwiches, 171
shiitake. *See* Shiitake
  mushrooms
Slow-Cooked Stuffing, 140
Tempeh and Tofu
  Hungarian Goulash,
  190–191
white. *See* White mushrooms

N
Napa cabbage, Cruciferous
  Vegetables, Tofu, and
  Rice, 177
Navy beans
  Black-Eyed Pea Chili, 115
  cook times for, 26
New potatoes. *See also*
  Potatoes
  Chunky Seitan Roast, 192
  "Meaty" Shiitake Stew, 112
Nonstick cooking sprays, 15
  "Cheesy" Cauliflower, 164
  Chocolaty Steel-
    Cut Oats, 40
  Chunky Seitan Roast, 192
  Coconutty Oats, 38
  Grains with Sesame
    Seeds, 136
  Hash-Brown Casserole, 41
  Italian Roasted Veggies, 154
  Macaroni Casserole
    Florentine, 143–144
  Mexican-Style
    Lasagna, 215–216
  Nontraditional Brown
    Betty, 236–237
  Peanut, Tempeh, and
    Butternut Squash
    Mole, 185–186
  Pear and Chocolate
    Cake, 232–233
  Pumpkin Cinnamon
    Rolls, 31–32

Pumpkin Gingerbread
  Cereal, 36–37
Pumpkin Pie, 229
Seitan and Sausage
  Cassoulet, 194
Slow-Baked Apples, 227
Southern-Style
  Casserole, 147–148
Super-Slow Tart Apple and
  Cinnamon Oatmeal, 39
Sweet Potato Casserole, 56
Nontraditional Antipasto,
  61–62
Nontraditional Brown Betty,
  236–237
Nutritional yeast
  Great Northern Bean
    "Chicken" Chili, 124
  Mac and Cheese, 142
Nuts
  cashews. *See* Cashews
  Nutty Coconut
    Curry Mix, 51
  peanuts. *See* Peanuts
  pecans. *See* Pecans
  walnuts. *See* Walnuts
Nutty Coconut Curry Mix, 51

O
Oats
  Chocolaty Steel-Cut Oats, 40
  Classic Apple Cobbler, 228
  Coconutty Oats, 38
  rolled. *See* Rolled oats
  steel-cut. *See* Steel-cut oats
  Super-Slow Tart Apple and
    Cinnamon Oatmeal, 39
Oil, olive. *See* Olive oil
Okra
  Eggplant, Okra, and
    Butternut Squash
    Stew, 167
  Lima Bean Gumbo, 149
Old-Fashioned Split Pea
  Soup, 69
Olive oil
  Bean and Penne
    Soup, 93–94
  Greens, Greens, Greens, 153
  Italian Oyster Mushrooms
    and Pilaf, 162

Jamaican Red Bean
   Soup, 95
A Little More than
   Split Pea Soup, 70
Mom's Vegetable
   Soup, 73–74
Nontraditional
   Antipasto, 61–62
Quinoa Chili, 121–122
Root Vegetables with
   Oil and Vinegar, 52
Split Mung Bean
   Soup, 83–84
Veggie and Chickpea
   Soup, 77–78
Olives
   black, Tempeh Enchilada
      Casserole, 187–188
   green, Eggplant and
      Capers, 156
Onions
   Alphabet Minestrone,
      2, 75–76
   Apples and Cabbage, 155
   Baked Bean Chili, 116
   Beans, Beans, and More
      Beans Soup, 92
   Black Bean and Chipotle
      Pepper Stew, 107
   Black Bean and
      Tomato Chili, 114
   Black Bean Soup, 85
   Black-Eyed Pea Chili, 115
   Carrot and Green Bean
      Casserole, 170
   Creamy Baked Potato
      and Veggie Soup, 96
   Easy Millet Stew, 101
   Frozen Veggie Stew, 99–100
   Great Northern Bean
      "Chicken" Chili, 124
   Lentil and Bean
      Stew, 108–109
   Lentil and Mushroom
      Soup, 87
   A Little More than
      Split Pea Soup, 70
   "Meaty" Shiitake Stew,
      112
   Mexican Bean Dip, 63
   Mexican-Style Dumpling
      Stew, 110–111

Mom's Vegetable
   Soup, 73–74
Moroccan-Style Lentil
   Soup, 90–91
Nontraditional
   Antipasto, 61–62
Old-Fashioned Beans
   and Weenies, 199
Pearl Barley and Lentil
   Soup, 88–89
precooking of, 11
red. See Red onions
scallions. See Scallions
Slow-Cooked Stuffing,
   140
Spiced Indian
   Chickpeas, 60
Spicy Pumpkin Chili, 123
Stuffed Picante Onions, 55
Sweet and Spicy
   Chickpea Stew, 102
Sweet Potato Chili, 120
Tomato Salsa, 58
Two-Bean Chili, 113
Veggie and Lentil Soup, 86
Veggie and Squash
   Stew, 106
white. See White onions
yellow. See Yellow onions
Orange juice, Two-Bean
   Chili, 113
Oranges
   Asian Potato Salad, 203
   juice. See Orange juice
   Mandarin Orange
      Vegetables and Rice, 128
Oyster mushrooms, Italian
   Oyster Mushrooms and
   Pilaf, 162

P
Parboiled rice, 23
Parmesan cheese, vegan
   Alphabet Minestrone,
      2, 75–76
   "Cheesy" Zucchini, Leeks,
      and Tomatoes, 159–160
   Creamy Baked Potato
      and Veggie Soup, 96
   Eggplant Parmesan, 172
Parsnips, Nontraditional
   Antipasto, 61–62

Pastas
   Alphabet Minestrone,
      2, 75–76
   Bean and Penne
      Soup, 93–94
   Fettuccine and
      Vegetables, 174
   Lentil Pasta Sauce, 141
   Mac and Cheese, 142
   Macaroni Casserole
      Florentine, 143–144
   precooking of, 15
   quinoa. See Quinoa
   Spaghetti and Hot Dogs, 146
   Tempeh and Tofu
      Hungarian Goulash,
      190–191
   Tofu and Spinach
      Lasagna, 183
   Vietnamese Noodle
      Soup, 204–205
   Who Needs Meat
      Meat Sauce, 198
Pea pods, Cruciferous
   Vegetables, Tofu, and
   Rice, 177
Peaches, Sweetened Fruit
   Curry, 217
Peanut butter
   Chocolate–Peanut Butter
      Cake, 2, 234–235
   Peanut, Tempeh, and
      Butternut Squash
      Mole, 185–186
Peanuts, Asian Fall Vegetable
   Stew, 208
Pearl barley
   Black Bean Breakfast
      Burritos, 2, 25, 42–43
   Pearl Barley and Lentil
      Soup, 88–89
Pearl onions, Nontraditional
   Antipasto, 61–62
Pearl tapioca, Extra-Creamy
   Tapioca Pudding, 33
Pears, Pear and Chocolate
   Cake, 232–233
Peas
   black-eyed. See Black-
      eyed peas
   Classic Veggies
      and Rice, 161

Peas (*continued*)
Drunken "Chicken" with
Brown Rice, 197
Frozen Veggie Stew, 99–100
Lentil and Bean
Stew, 108–109
Mom's Vegetable
Soup, 73–74
Old-Fashioned Split
Pea Soup, 69
Portobello Mushroom and
Tempeh Stroganoff, 189
snow. *See* Snow peas
split peas. *See* Split peas
Veggie Bake, 173
Pecans
Nontraditional Brown
Betty, 236–237
Slow-Baked Apples, 227
Spicy Pecans, 50
Super-Slow Tart Apple and
Cinnamon Oatmeal, 39
Sweet Potato Casserole, 56
Penne pasta, Bean and Penne
Soup, 93–94
Peppers
bell. *See* Bell peppers
chiles. *See* Chiles
chipotle. *See* Chipotle
peppers
jalepeño. *See* Jalepeño
peppers
Picante sauce, Spicy Lentils,
139
Pies, Pumpkin Pie, 229
Pilaf-style rice. *See also* Rice
Italian Oyster Mushrooms
and Pilaf, 162
Spicy Lentils, 139
Pineapple
Barbecue-Style Tofu and
Pineapple, 180–181
Easy Millet Stew, 101
Sweetened Fruit Curry, 217
Pinto beans
cook times for, 26
Moroccan-Style Lentil
Soup, 90–91
Southern-Style
Casserole, 147–148
Spicy Vegan Chili, 119
Two-Bean Chili, 113

Plum tomatoes. *See also*
Tomatoes
Eggplant and Capers, 156
Tomato Salsa, 58
Who Needs Meat
Meat Sauce, 198
Polenta, Polenta and Bean
Casserole, 168–169
Portobello mushrooms. *See*
also Mushrooms
Portobello Mushroom and
Tempeh Stroganoff, 189
Portobello Mushroom
Submarine
Sandwiches, 171
Potatoes
Asian Potato Salad, 203
Chunky Seitan Roast, 192
Classic Veggies
and Rice, 161
Creamy Baked Potato
and Veggie Soup, 96
Creamy Curry Stew, 103–104
Creamy Pumpkin Stew, 105
Easy Millet Stew, 101
Frozen Veggie Stew, 99–100
Hash-Brown Casserole, 41
Hearty Stew, 195
Italian Roasted Veggies, 154
Kidney Beans Curry and
Basmati Rice, 221
"Meaty" Shiitake Stew, 112
Mom's Vegetable
Soup, 73–74
new. *See* New potatoes
Old-Fashioned Split
Pea Soup, 69
red. *See* Red potatoes
sweet. *See* Sweet potatoes
Tempeh and Tofu Hungarian
Goulash, 190–191
as thickener, 10
Powdered sugar, Spicy Pecans,
50
Precooking tips, 11
Preparation tips
for arborio rice, 23–24
for bell peppers, 11
for nonstick cooking
spray, 15
for vegetable broth, 21–22
for vegetables, 11

Prunes, Root Vegetables and
Dried Fruit, 158
Pudding
Arborio Rice, 23–24
Extra-Creamy Tapioca
Pudding, 33
Rice Pudding, 226
Pumpkin
Creamy Pumpkin Stew,
105
Pumpkin Cinnamon
Rolls, 2, 31–32
Pumpkin Gingerbread
Cereal, 36–37
Pumpkin Pie, 229
Spicy Pumpkin Chili, 123
Puréed vegetables, as
thickener, 10

Q
Quinoa
Banana Quinoa
Breakfast, 34
Black Bean and Chipotle
Pepper Stew, 107
Lentil and Bean
Stew, 108–109
Mac and Cheese, 142
Quinoa Chili, 121–122

R
Raisins
Amaranth and Fruit, 35
Eggplant, Okra, and
Butternut Squash
Stew, 167
Super-Slow Tart Apple and
Cinnamon Oatmeal, 39
Rataouille Niçoise, 2, 157
Red beans
Bean Smorgasbord, 138
Jamaican Red Bean Soup, 95
Red bell peppers. *See also* Bell
peppers
Bean and Penne
Soup, 93–94
Creamy Curry Stew,
103–104
Italian Oyster Mushrooms
and Pilaf, 162
Mom's Vegetable
Soup, 73–74

Nontraditional
Antipasto, 61–62
Quinoa Chili, 121–122
Rataouille Niçoise, 2, 157
Stuffed Picante Onions, 55
Two-Bean Chili, 113
Red chiles. *See also* Chiles
Spiced Indian
Chickpeas, 60
Vietnamese Noodle
Soup, 204–205
Red lentils
Lentil and Bean
Stew, 108–109
Red onions. *See also* Onions
Barley and Beans, 134
Black Bean and Chipotle
Pepper Stew, 107
Black Bean and
Tomato Chili, 114
Black Bean Soup, 85
Greens, Greens, Greens, 153
Italian Roasted Veggies, 154
Sweet Potato Chili, 120
Red potatoes. *See also*
Potatoes
Italian Roasted Veggies, 154
Mexican-Style
Minestrone, 210
Mom's Vegetable
Soup, 73–74
Red wine vinegar
Black Bean Soup, 85
Eggplant and Capers, 156
Refried beans (vegan),
Enchilada Wraps, 2, 213
Rice
arborio, 23–24. *See
also* Arborio rice
Beans and Molasses, 135
brown. *See* Brown rice
Cajun-Style Kidney
Beans and Rice, 132
cereal, Nutty Coconut
Curry Mix, 51
"Chicken" Chow Mein, 209
Chickpea Coconut
Curry, 220
Chinese Hot Pot, 206–207
Classic Veggies
and Rice, 161
converted (parboiled), 23

Crispy Tofu and Brown
Basmati Rice, 178–179
Cruciferous Vegetables,
Tofu, and Rice, 177
Curried Rice and
Lentils, 222
Enchilada Wraps, 2, 213
Grains with Sesame
Seeds, 136
Italian Oyster Mushrooms
and Pilaf, 162
Kidney Beans Curry and
Basmati Rice, 221
long-grain. *See* Long-
grain rice
Mandarin Orange
Vegetables and Rice, 128
Mexican Beans
and Rice, 131
Mexican Rice with Black
Beans and Salsa, 211–212
noodles, Vietnamese
Noodle Soup, 204–205
Pilaf-Style Rice, 23
preparation instructions
for, 22–24
pudding, 23–24
Rice Pudding, 226
shortcuts for, 19, 22–24
Spanish Rice and
Black Beans, 130
Spicy Lentils, 139
Spinach and Yellow Rice, 129
as thickener, 10, 22
Vegan Risotto, 145
Rice vinegar, Hot and Sour
Soup, 60
Risotto
Arborio Rice, 23–24
Vegan Risotto, 145
Roasted vegetables, Italian
Roasted Veggies, 154
Rolled oats, Classic Apple
Cobbler, 228
Rolls, Pumpkin Cinnamon
Rolls, 2, 31–32
Romaine lettuce, Asian
Potato Salad, 203
Root vegetables
Nontraditional
Antipasto, 61–62
preparation tips for, 11

Root Vegetables and
Dried Fruit, 158
Root Vegetables with
Oil and Vinegar, 52
Rutabaga and Cabbage
Stew, 165–166
Rum, Nontraditional Brown
Betty, 236–237
Russet potatoes
Creamy Baked Potato
and Veggie Soup, 96
Rutabagas, Rutabaga and
Cabbage Stew, 165–166

S
Saffron threads, Spinach and
Yellow Rice, 129
Salads
Asian Potato Salad, 203
Nontraditional
Antipasto, 61–62
Salsas
Black Bean Breakfast
Burritos, 2, 25, 42–43
Black Bean Tacos, 214
Hash-Brown Casserole, 41
Meaty Seitan Tacos, 193
Mexican Rice with Black
Beans and Salsa,
211–212
Mexican-Style
Lasagna, 215–216
Spanish Rice and
Black Beans, 130
Tempeh Enchilada
Casserole, 187–188
Tomato Salsa, 58
Salt, seasoned. *See* Seasoned
salt
Sambal oelek, Asian Fall
Vegetable Stew, 208
Sandwiches
Enchilada Wraps, 2, 21
Portobello Mushroom
Submarine
Sandwiches, 171
Sauces
adobo. *See* Adobo sauce
Asian chili sauce, Hot
and Sour Soup, 67
Butterscotch Sauce, 225
hoisin. *See* Hoisin sauce

Sauces (*continued*)
    picante. *See* Picante sauce
    tabasco. *See* Tabasco sauce
Sausage (vegan), Seitan and
    Sausage Cassoulet, 194
Scallions
    Black Bean Breakfast
        Burritos, 2, 25, 42–43
    Black-Eyed Pea Chili, 115
    "Chicken" Chow Mein, 209
    Chinese Hot Pot, 206–207
    Creamy Baked Potato
        and Veggie Soup, 96
    Fettuccine and
        Vegetables, 174
    Jamaican Red Bean
        Soup, 95
    Vietnamese Noodle
        Soup, 204–205
Seasoned salt, Curried
    Almonds, 49
Seaweed. *See* Kombu seaweed
Seitan
    Chunky Seitan Roast, 3, 192
    definition of, 2
    Hearty Stew, 195
    Meaty Seitan Tacos, 193
    Seitan and Sausage
        Cassoulet, 194
    shortcuts for, 24
    Slow-Cooked Seitan, 24–25
    uses of, 2–3
Sesame seeds, Grains with
    Sesame Seeds, 136
Shiitake mushrooms. *See also*
    Mushrooms
    Asian Fall Vegetable
        Stew, 208
    Chinese Hot Pot, 206–207
    Hot and Sour Soup, 67
    "Meaty" Shiitake
        Stew, 2, 112
Shortcuts, 17–27
    beans, 25–27
    grains, 24–25
    overviews of, 19
    rice, 22–24
    stock *vs.* broth, 19–20, 19–21
Sloppy Joes
    Tofu Sloppy Joes, 182
    Tofu-Free Sloppy Joes, 200
Slow cookers
    cleaning of, 9

food amounts in, 15
    new *vs.* older, 8
    selection criteria for, 8–9
    sizes of, 8
    variations in, 9
Slow cooking
    advantages of, 1–3, 7
    breakfasts, 29–43
    building blocks of, 19
    cooking time
        considerations, 15
    desserts, 223–237
    herbs, fresh *vs.* dried, 11–12
    in high altitudes, 15
    meat alternatives, 175–200
    nonstick cooking
        sprays and, 15
    overviews of, 1–3, 7–15
    safety considerations for, 7–8
    serving size variations
        and, 9
    shortcuts for, 17–27
    slow cookers. *See*
        Slow cookers
    snacks-sides-
        appetizers, 45–63
    soups, 65–96
    stews and chilies, 97–124
    thickeners and, 10
    time management
        considerations for, 11
    vegetables, preparation
        tips for, 11
Slow-Cooked Beans, 26–27
Slow-Cooked Brown Basmati
    Rice, 22–23
Slow-Cooked Seitan, 24–25
Slow-Cooked Stuffing, 140
Smoke, liquid. *See* Liquid
    smoke
Snacks-sides-appetizers,
    45–63
    Apricot Butter, 47
    Curried Almonds, 49
    Home-Style Applesauce, 48
    Marinated Mushrooms, 59
    Mashed Cauliflower and
        Garlic "Potatoes," 2, 57
    Mexican Bean Dip, 63
    Nutty Coconut
        Curry Mix, 51
    Root Vegetables with
        Oil and Vinegar, 52

Spiced Indian
    Chickpeas, 60
Spicy Pecans, 50
Stuffed Picante Onions, 55
Sweet Acorn Squash, 53–54
Sweet Potato Casserole, 56
Tomato Salsa, 58
Snow peas, Chinese Hot Pot,
    206–207
Soaking process, beans, 26
Soft vegetables, preparation
    tips for, 11
Soups, 67–96
    Alphabet Minestrone,
        2, 75–76
    Bean and Penne
        Soup, 93–94
    Beans, Beans, and More
        Beans Soup, 92
    Black Bean Soup, 85
    Coconut, Squash, and
        Tofu Soup, 82
    Creamy Baked Potato
        and Veggie Soup, 96
    Creamy Butternut
        Squash Soup, 71–72
    Creamy Chickpea
        Soup, 80–81
    Farro and Split Pea
        Soup, 127
    Garlicky Tomato Soup, 68
    Hot and Sour Soup, 67
    Jamaican Red Bean Soup, 95
    Lentil and Mushroom
        Soup, 87
    A Little More than
        Split Pea Soup, 70
    Mexican-Style
        Minestrone, 210
    Mom's Vegetable
        Soup, 73–74
    Moroccan-Style Lentil
        Soup, 90–91
    Old-Fashioned Split
        Pea Soup, 69
    Pearl Barley and Lentil
        Soup, 88–89
    stews. *See* Stews and chilies
    Veggie and Chickpea
        Soup, 77–78
    Veggie and Lentil Soup, 86
    Vietnamese Noodle
        Soup, 204–205

Sour cream, vegan
    Black Bean and
        Tomato Chili, 114
    Hash-Brown Casserole, 41
    Mexican-Style
        Lasagna, 215–216
    Spicy Vegan Chili, 119
    Sweet Potato Chili, 120
    Southern-Style Casserole,
        147–148
Soy crumbles
    Stuffed Bell Peppers, 196
    Who Needs Meat
        Meat Sauce, 198
Soy ice cream
    Fudgy Brownies, 230
    Slow-Baked Apples, 227
Soy milk
    Fudgy Brownies, 230
    Mashed Cauliflower and
        Garlic "Potatoes," 2, 57
    Pumpkin Gingerbread
        Cereal, 36–37
    Rice Pudding, 226
    Super-Slow Tart Apple and
        Cinnamon Oatmeal, 39
    Sweet Potato Casserole, 56
Soy-based products
    creamer, Butterscotch
        Sauce, 225
    crumbles. See Soy crumbles
    ice cream. See Soy ice cream
    milk. See Soy milk
    tempeh, 2–3. See
        also Tempeh
    tofu, 2–3. See also Tofu
Spaghetti. See also Pastas
    Spaghetti and Hot Dogs,
        146
    Who Needs Meat
        Meat Sauce, 198
Spanish Rice and Black Beans,
    130
Spiced Indian Chickpeas, 60
Spicy Pecans, 50
Spicy Pumpkin Chili, 123
Spicy Vegan Chili, 119
Spinach
    Polenta and Bean
        Casserole, 168–169
    precooking of, 15
    Spinach and Yellow
        Rice, 129

Split Mung Bean
    Soup, 83–84
    Tofu and Spinach
        Lasagna, 183
Split mung beans, Split Mung
    Bean Soup, 83–84
Split peas
    cook times for, 26
    Farro and Split Pea
        Soup, 127
    A Little More than
        Split Pea Soup, 70
    Old-Fashioned Split
        Pea Soup, 69
Sprays, cooking. See Nonstick
    cooking sprays
Sprouts. See Bean sprouts
Squash
    carnival. See Carnival
        squash
    Coconut, Squash, and
        Tofu Soup, 82
    Creamy Butternut
        Squash Soup, 71–72
    Fettuccine and
        Vegetables, 174
    Kidney Bean and Barley
        Stuffed Squash, 163
    summer. See Summer
        squash
    Sweet Acorn Squash, 53–54
    Veggie and Squash
        Stew, 106
    yellow crookneck. See
        Yellow crookneck squash
Star anise, Vietnamese
    Noodle Soup, 204–205
Steel-cut oats, Chocolaty
    Steel-Cut Oats, 40
Stews and chilies, 97–124
    Asian Fall Vegetable
        Stew, 208
    Baked Bean Chili, 116
    Black Bean and Chipotle
        Pepper Stew, 107
    Black Bean and
        Tomato Chili, 114
    Black-Eyed Pea Chili, 115
    Creamy Curry Stew,
        103–104
    Creamy Pumpkin Stew, 105
    Easy Millet Stew, 101
    Frozen Veggie Stew, 99–100

Great Northern Bean
    "Chicken" Chili, 124
    Hearty Stew, 195
    Lentil and Bean
        Stew, 108–109
    Lima Bean Chili, 117–118
    "Meaty" Shiitake
        Stew, 2, 112
    Mexican-Style Dumpling
        Stew, 110–111
    Quinoa Chili, 121–122
    Rutabaga and Cabbage
        Stew, 165–166
    Spicy Pumpkin Chili, 123
    Spicy Vegan Chili, 119
    Sweet and Spicy
        Chickpea Stew, 102
    Sweet Potato Chili, 120
    Two-Bean Chili, 113
    vegetables, preparation
        tips for, 11
    Veggie and Squash
        Stew, 106
Stuffed Bell Peppers, 196
Stuffed Picante Onions, 55
Substitutes, eggs. See Egg
    substitutes
Sugar, brown. See Brown
    sugar
Summer squash, Fettuccine
    and Vegetables, 174
Sunflower seeds, Kidney
    Bean and Barley Stuffed
    Squash, 163
Super-Slow Tart Apple and
    Cinnamon Oatmeal, 39
Sweet Acorn Squash, 53–54
Sweet and Spicy Chickpea
    Stew, 102
Sweet potatoes
    Asian Fall Vegetable
        Stew, 208
    Lentil and Bean
        Stew, 108–109
    Sweet and Spicy
        Chickpea Stew, 102
    Sweet Potato and Apple
        Curry, 218–219
    Sweet Potato Casserole, 56
    Sweet Potato Chili, 120
Sweetened Fruit Curry, 217
Syrup, maple. See Maple
    syrup

T

Tabasco sauce, Curried Rice
    and Lentils, 222
Tacos
    Black Beans Tacos, 214
    Meaty Seitan Tacos, 193
Tahini, Mac and Cheese, 142
Tamari
    Barbecue-Style Tofu and
        Pineapple, 180–181
    Chinese Hot Pot, 206–207
    Kidney Bean and Barley
        Stuffed Squash, 163
    Rutabaga and Cabbage
        Stew, 165–166
Tapioca
    Carrot and Green Bean
        Casserole, 170
    Extra-Creamy Tapioca
        Pudding, 33
Tapioca starch, as thickener,
    10
Tempeh
    definition of, 2–3
    Peanut, Tempeh, and
        Butternut Squash
        Mole, 185–186
    Portobello Mushroom and
        Tempeh Stroganoff, 189
    Tempeh and Tofu
        Hungarian Goulash,
        190–191
    Tempeh Enchilada
        Casserole, 2, 187–188
    Tempeh with Almond
        Butter, 184
    uses of, 2–3
Thickeners, 10
Tofu
    Barbecue-Style Tofu and
        Pineapple, 180–181
    Chinese Hot Pot, 206–207
    Coconut, Squash, and
        Tofu Soup, 82
    Crispy Tofu and Brown
        Basmati Rice, 178–179
    Cruciferous Vegetables,
        Tofu, and Rice, 177
    definition of, 2
    Hot and Sour Soup, 67
    Tempeh and Tofu Hungarian
        Goulash, 190–191

Tofu and Spinach
    Lasagna, 183
Tofu Sloppy Joes, 182
    uses of, 2–3
Tofu-Free Sloppy Joes, 200
Tomatoes, 108–109
    Alphabet Minestrone,
        2, 75–76
    Baked Bean Chili, 116
    Barley and Beans, 134
    Bean and Penne
        Soup, 93–94
    Beans, Beans, and More
        Beans Soup, 92
    Black Bean and Chipotle
        Pepper Stew, 107
    Black Bean and
        Tomato Chili, 114
    Black Bean Breakfast
        Burritos, 2, 25, 42–43
    Black Bean Soup, 85
    Black Bean Tacos, 214
    "Cheesy" Zucchini, Leeks,
        and Tomatoes, 159–160
    Chickpea Couscous, 133
    Classic Veggies and Rice, 161
    Creamy Chickpea
        Soup, 80–81
    Eggplant and Capers, 156
    Garlicky Tomato Soup, 68
    Italian Oyster Mushrooms
        and Pilaf, 162
    Kidney Beans Curry and
        Basmati Rice, 221
    Lentil Pasta Sauce, 141
    Lima Bean Chili, 117–118
    Lima Bean Gumbo, 149
    "Meaty" Shiitake Stew, 112
    Mexican Bean Dip, 63
    Mexican Beans
        and Rice, 131
    Mexican Black-
        Eyed Peas, 137
    Mexican-Style Dumpling
        Stew, 110–111
    Mexican-Style
        Minestrone, 210
    Peanut, Tempeh, and
        Butternut Squash
        Mole, 185–186
    Pearl Barley and Lentil
        Soup, 88–89

plum. *See* Plum tomatoes
    Polenta and Bean
        Casserole, 168–169
    Quinoa Chili, 121–122
    Rataouille Niçoise, 2, 157
    Seitan and Sausage
        Cassoulet, 194
    Spanish Rice and
        Black Beans, 130
    Spiced Indian
        Chickpeas, 60
    Spicy Lentils, 139
    Spicy Pumpkin Chili, 123
    Spicy Vegan Chili, 119
    Stuffed Bell Peppers, 196
    Tofu-Free Sloppy Joes, 200
    Tomato Salsa, 58
    Two-Bean Chili, 113
    Veggie and Chickpea
        Soup, 77–78
    Veggie and Lentil Soup, 86
    Veggie and Squash
        Stew, 106
    Veggie Bake, 173
    Who Needs Meat
        Meat Sauce, 198
Tortillas
    Black Bean Breakfast
        Burritos, 2, 25, 42–43
    Enchilada Wraps, 2, 213
    Tempeh Enchilada
        Casserole, 187–188
Tropical fruit cocktail,
    Sweetened Fruit Curry,
    217
Turnips
    Root Vegetables and
        Dried Fruit, 158
    Root Vegetables with
        Oil and Vinegar, 52
Two-Bean Chili, 113

V

Vegetable boullion cubes,
    shortcuts for, 19
Vegetable dishes, 151–174
    Apples and Cabbage, 155
    Asian Fall Vegetable
        Stew, 208
    Carrot and Green Bean
        Casserole, 170
    "Cheesy" Cauliflower, 164

"Cheesy" Zucchini, Leeks,
and Tomatoes, 159–160
Classic Veggies
and Rice, 161
Creamy Baked Potato
and Veggie Soup, 96
Cruciferous Vegetables,
Tofu, and Rice, 177
Eggplant and Capers, 156
Eggplant, Okra, and
Butternut Squash
Stew, 167
Eggplant Parmesan, 172
Fettuccine Vegetables, 174
Frozen Veggie Stew, 99–100
Greens, Greens, Greens, 153
Italian Oyster Mushrooms
and Pilaf, 162
Italian Roasted Veggies, 154
Kidney Bean and Barley
Stuffed Squash, 163
Mandarin Orange
Vegetables and Rice, 128
Mom's Vegetable
Soup, 73–74
Polenta and Bean
Casserole, 168–169
Portobello Mushroom
Submarine
Sandwiches, 171
Rataouille Niçoise, 2, 157
Root Vegetables and
Dried Fruit, 158
Rutabaga and Cabbage
Stew, 165–166
vegetable dishes. See
Vegetable dishes
Veggie and Chickpea
Soup, 77–78
Veggie and Lentil Soup, 86
Veggie and Squash
Stew, 106
Veggie Bake, 173
Vegetable stock
Alphabet Minestrone,
2, 75–76
Apples and Cabbage, 155
Bean and Penne
Soup, 93–94
Beans, Beans, and More
Beans Soup, 92

Black Bean and Chipotle
Pepper Stew, 107
Black Bean Breakfast
Burritos, 2, 25, 42–43
Black Bean Soup, 85
Black-Eyed Pea Chili, 115
Creamy Baked Potato
and Veggie Soup, 96
Creamy Butternut
Squash Soup, 71–72
Creamy Chickpea
Soup, 80–81
Creamy Pumpkin Stew, 105
Easy Millet Stew, 101
Eggplant, Okra, and
Butternut Squash
Stew, 167
Farro and Split Pea
Soup, 127
Frozen Veggie Stew, 99–100
Garlicky Tomato Soup, 68
Great Northern Bean
"Chicken" Chili, 124
Greens, Greens, Greens, 153
Hot and Sour Soup, 67
Jamaican Red Bean
Soup, 95
Kidney Bean and Barley
Stuffed Squash, 163
Lima Bean Chili, 117–118
A Little More than
Split Pea Soup, 70
"Meaty" Shiitake Stew, 112
Mexican-Style Dumpling
Stew, 110–111
Moroccan-Style Lentil
Soup, 90–91
Old-Fashioned Split
Pea Soup, 69
Peanut, Tempeh, and
Butternut Squash
Mole, 185–186
Pearl Barley and Lentil
Soup, 88–89
Quinoa Chili, 121–122
Rataouille Niçoise, 2, 157
Root Vegetables and
Dried Fruit, 158
Rutabaga and Cabbage
Stew, 165–166
Spicy Vegan Chili, 119

Split Mung Bean
Soup, 83–84
Veggie and Chickpea
Soup, 77–78
Veggie and Lentil Soup, 86
Veggie and Squash
Stew, 106
Vietnamese Noodle
Soup, 204–205
Vegetables
precooking of, 11
preparation tips for, 11
shortcuts for, 19
vegetable dishes. See
Vegetable dishes
vegetable stock. See
Vegetable stock
Veggie and Chickpea Soup,
77–78
Veggie and Lentil Soup, 86
Veggie and Squash Stew, 106
Veggie Bake, 173
Veggie crumbles, Stuffed Bell
Peppers, 196
Vietnamese Noodle Soup,
204–205
Vinegar
balsamic. See Balsamic
vinegar
red wine. See Red
wine vinegar
rice. See Rice vinegar

W
Walnuts
Banana Quinoa
Breakfast, 34
Super-Slow Tart Apple and
Cinnamon Oatmeal, 39
Sweet Acorn Squash, 53–54
Water chestnuts
"Chicken" Chow Mein, 209
Chinese Hot Pot, 206–207
Crispy Tofu and Brown
Basmati Rice, 178–179
Wheat Meat. See Seitan
White beans
Lentil and Bean
Stew, 108–109
Lima Bean Chili, 117–118

White beans (*continued*)
    Macaroni Casserole
        Florentine, 143–144
    Mom's Vegetable
        Soup, 73–74
    Seitan and Sausage
        Cassoulet, 194
White chickpeas. *See*
    Chickpeas
White miso paste
    Macaroni Casserole
        Florentine, 143–144
    Vietnamese Noodle
        Soup, 204–205
White mushrooms. *See also*
    Mushrooms
    "Cheesy" Cauliflower, 164
    Easy Millet Stew, 101
    Fettuccine and
        Vegetables, 174
    Lentil and Bean
        Stew, 108–109
    Tempeh and Tofu Hungarian
        Goulash, 190–191
White onions. *See also* Onions
    Creamy Baked Potato
        and Veggie Soup, 96
    Drunken "Chicken" with
        Brown Rice, 197
    Lentil and Bean
        Stew, 108–109
    "Meaty" Shiitake Stew, 112
    Nontraditional
        Antipasto, 61–62
    Stuffed Picante Onions, 55
White rice, Spinach and
    Yellow Rice, 129
Who Needs Meat Meat Sauce,
    198
Whole-wheat bread crumbs,
    Slow-Cooked Stuffing,
    140
Wild mushrooms, Lentil and
    Mushroom Soup, 87
Wraps, Enchilada Wraps, 2,
    213

Y
Yeast, nutritional. *See*
    Nutritional yeast
Yellow bell peppers. *See also*
    Bell peppers
    Crispy Tofu and Brown
        Basmati Rice, 178–179
    Tofu-Free Sloppy Joes, 200
Yellow crookneck squash,
    Rataouille Niçoise, 2, 157
Yellow onions. *See also*
    Onions
    Alphabet Minestrone,
        2, 75–76
    Baked Bean Chili, 116
    Beans, Beans, and More
        Beans Soup, 92
    Black-Eyed Pea Chili, 115
    "Cheesy" Cauliflower, 164
    Easy Millet Stew, 101
    Eggplant and Capers, 156
    Eggplant, Okra, and
        Butternut Squash
        Stew, 167
    Frozen Veggie Stew, 99–100
    Great Northern Bean
        "Chicken" Chili, 124
    Italian Oyster Mushrooms
        and Pilaf, 162
    Lentil and Mushroom
        Soup, 87
    Lima Bean Gumbo, 149
    A Little More than
        Split Pea Soup, 70
    Mexican-Style Dumpling
        Stew, 110–111
    Mom's Vegetable
        Soup, 73–74
    Moroccan-Style Lentil
        Soup, 90–91
    Pearl Barley and Lentil
        Soup, 88–89
    Rataouille Niçoise, 2, 157
    Root Vegetables and
        Dried Fruit, 158

Rutabaga and Cabbage
    Stew, 165–166
Seitan and Sausage
    Cassoulet, 194
Spiced Indian
    Chickpeas, 60
Spicy Pumpkin Chili, 123
Stuffed Picante Onions, 55
Sweet and Spicy
    Chickpea Stew, 102
Tofu Sloppy Joes, 182
Tomato Salsa, 58
Two-Bean Chili, 113
Veggie and Lentil Soup, 86
Veggie and Squash
    Stew, 106
Who Needs Meat
    Meat Sauce, 198

Z
Zucchini
    Alphabet Minestrone,
        2, 75–76
    "Cheesy" Zucchini, Leeks,
        and Tomatoes, 159–160
    Classic Veggies
        and Rice, 161
    Eggplant and Capers, 156
    Eggplant, Okra, and
        Butternut Squash
        Stew, 167
    Fettuccine Vegetables, 174
    Italian Roasted Veggies, 154
    Lentil and Bean
        Stew, 108–109
    Mandarin Orange
        Vegetables and Rice, 128
    preparation tips for, 11
    Spaghetti and Hot Dogs, 146
    Veggie and Chickpea
        Soup, 77–78
    Veggie and Squash
        Stew, 106

Made in the USA
San Bernardino, CA
30 August 2018